I Reminisce

E. Roland Harriman seated at desk in Partners' Room,
Brown Brothers Harriman & Co., about 1965.

I REMINISCE

by E. Roland Harriman

Doubleday & Company, Inc.
Garden City, New York 1975

ISBN: 0-385-11469-9
Library of Congress Catalog Card Number 75–21875
Copyright © 1975 by E. Roland Harriman
All Rights Reserved
Printed in the United States of America
First Edition

CONTENTS

I: WAY BACK YONDER   1

II: GROWING UP   27

III: BOATS, BUGS, BRIDGES AND BOYS   53

IV: MY FAVORITE PEOPLE   73

V: CRISIS—CRISIS—CRISIS   95

VI: ONE WAY TO RUN A RAILROAD I   117

VII: ONE WAY TO RUN A RAILROAD II   133

VIII: TRAVELS AND ADVENTURES   153

IX: THE GOOD NEIGHBOR I   185

X: THE GOOD NEIGHBOR II   207

XI: THE COMEBACK OF A SPORT   227

XII: PARADISE   253

I Reminisce

CHAPTER I: WAY BACK YONDER

One day in the first decade of our twentieth century, the naturalist John Muir was chatting with my father, Edward Henry Harriman, about the troubles he was having getting started with a new book. According to Muir, my father said, "I will show you how to write books. The trouble with you is that you're too slow in your beginnings. You plan and brood too much. Begin! Begin! Put forth what you wish to say in the first words that come to mind, just as you talk, so that all that is to go in the book is got down."

If the tone of these reminiscences might seem relaxed and easygoing, I would therefore cite distinguished precedent. And if the writing comes across as conversational, I have just one excuse. It is that my wife, most importantly, and some of my partners asked me simply to jot down some of my reminiscences. I have therefore had a very long conversation with a tape recorder. And it is true, as they say, that you can remember much more about your childhood than you can about last week. So— begin, begin, begin.

I might say that it all started on Christmas Eve, 1895, in an old brownstone house at 22 East Fifty-first Street, in New York City. That was a side street stepsister of the rather magnificent complex of brownstones situated right back of St. Patrick's Cathedral. And, about being born on Christmas Eve, everybody used to say, "You poor boy, you only get one present—for Christmas and for your birthday," and they must have felt sorry for me because they would always get me the two presents and I would always do very well.

The only disadvantage about being born on Christmas Eve that I can recall is that I had three names. These were Edward, Roland and Noel. The Edward was after my father, the Roland was a corruption of a Harriman family name, Orlando, and Noel was tacked on to celebrate a Christmas baby. Well, I had a lot of trouble. I used to abbreviate to E. R. N. Harriman and that looked awful. Then I called myself Edward R. Harriman, to indicate that I was my father's son. And then, I thought, you do not want just to hang onto your father's reputation, so I converted my name to E. Roland Harriman. So that is the way it has been.

My most memorable Christmas, in fact, concerned the feeling there was between my father and myself. I was ten years old, and for several years I had considered myself handy with tools, carpenters' tools in particular. I had made lopsided birdhouses, stern-wheeled flatboats powered by elastic bands, and all the other knickknacks that used to be a joy to the young in that first decade. My toy instruments never cut true, however, and I blamed them instead of myself. I was convinced that, with a proper set of tools, I was destined to be a master carpenter and a builder of objects of beauty.

Time and again, as Christmastime rolled around, I had asked my father for a chest of tools worthy of my skill. Year after year, Santa Claus brought me presents galore to delight any child, and birthday presents, too. But no tools. "Boy," my father would say, "remember, a good workman can work with poor tools." Wise words, but no great consolation to a disappointed youngster.

But that Christmas there it was, and from the size and shape of the bulky box, it could be nothing else. Oblivious to all the family and to the surplusage of other presents, I threw open the chest.

Yes, there they were! Real saws, crosscut and rip, man-sized hammers, brace and bits, chisels, gouges, planes and all the other tools of the trade. Enough to build a house—but the next spring I settled for a chicken coop. Longer than the tools, my father's words remained with me and stood me in good stead for threescore years, "Boy, remember, a good workman can work with poor tools."

Actually, the first thing I distinctly remember—some six years before that—was a crateful of squawking chickens dropped into the water between a steamship and a dock, and thereby hangs another tale. In 1899, my father's physicians advised him to take a rest, as he had been working very hard in the reorganization of the Union Pacific Railroad. His idea of a rest was to charter a steamship out of Seattle and take a group of distinguished scientists on a three-month jaunt along the Alaska shore, and that is where the chickens came in.

I was standing at the rail of the steamship at Seattle, watching the last-minute preparations before departure,

3

and among other things some live poultry, pigs and even a cow were put on board. The reason for the cow was to produce milk for one young passenger, Roland. Well, one of the crates of chickens slipped out of the net and into the water and that is what I first remember in life. The desperation of those chickens! Fortunately, I am glad to say, they were rescued, and they and their eggs were eaten on the trip.

For me, the most important thing about the trip was that my father took me along. I vaguely remember walking along the deck with my father one day, pulling a miniature Eskimo canoe on a string. I vaguely remember running onto an uncharted reef in the middle of the night and the tide came up, and we got off all right. It was a famous trip, taken in conjunction with the Smithsonian Institution, and there were a lot of famous scientists on board—a chief botanist, geologist and all the other top -ists that existed at that time.

My father organized things so that the scientists could be dropped off at various points along the coastline, with the equipment they needed to make their explorations and studies. Then he would go on, drop off somebody else, come back and pick up the first bunch and so on. We even landed in another continent—on the Siberian coast, at a place called Plover Bay.

Many years later, my brother, Averell, then our Ambassador to Moscow, was able to tell a startled Stalin that the first time he ever landed in Russia was without a passport.

We were on a star trip, as I now know, and the Smithsonian published twelve volumes on it. The first two were a narrative of the trip itself. The other ten were written

4

by the various scientists who made up the passenger list. The natural history collections from the trip included thirteen genera and six hundred species that were new to science. There were also five thousand photographs, considered to be the best ever taken of the Alaska coast up to that time, and many sketches and paintings by the famous artists who accompanied us.

My father, I was reminded for many years, attained his own objective, and shot an enormous Kodiak bear whose skin graced our parlor floor. It was the only bear secured by the expedition and was the first animal of this particular species that had ever been measured and photographed.

I am even more indebted to John Muir, however, and not for the first time, for a very human glimpse of my father. Muir commented, "Before I came to know him, I thought like many others that money-making might be one of the springs of his action. One evening, when the Alaskan expedition was at Kodiak, the scientists assembled on the forecastle awaiting the dinner bell, began to talk of the blessed ministry of wealth, especially in Mr. Harriman's case, now that some of it was being devoted to science.

"When these wealth laudations were sounding loudest, I teasingly interrupted them, saying, 'I don't think Mr. Harriman is very rich. He has not as much money as I have. I have all I want, and Mr. Harriman has not.' This saying somehow reached Mr. Harriman's ear and, after dinner, seating himself beside me, he said, 'I have never cared for money except as power to put to work. I was lucky and my friends and neighbors, observing my luck, brought their money to me to invest, and in this

5

way I have come to handle large sums. What I most enjoy is the power of creation, getting into partnership with nature and doing good, helping to feed man and beast, and making everybody and everything a little better and happier.'"

I was the youngest son of what nowadays would be regarded as a large family. I had an older brother named Harry, who died before I was born. He died of diphtheria in the year before they found a cure for it. My sister Mary was the eldest, and she was fourteen years older than me. Then came Cornelia, then Carol and then Averell, who was four years my senior.

As I was the youngest, all the others were convinced that I was being spoiled by my mother, which was probably true, and they did not let me enjoy this very much. They would take out of me what my mother pushed into me! But it was really a great experience for me to have this type of family, because I saw so many members of different generations. When you are a youngster, fourteen years is a lifetime. And I got to know an extraordinary group of people, and these were often friends of my sisters.

I might mention right here that my sister Mary was really a very valuable member of the community. The year she made her debut she decided there was an awful lot of froufrou, a lot of unnecessary expenses, the money for which could be put to better use. She loved company, she loved to dance, she loved great fun. She had a laugh that was most infectious. And she talked to a few of her co-debutantes, and they decided they should do something more with their youth. To make a long story short, one result was the founding of the Junior League.

All the girls looked different. Mary was dark, very attractive, and Cornelia was a very lovely blond girl, as she was all through her life. Carol was also fair-haired, very handsome.

As for brother Averell, there will be much to tell throughout these reminiscences. During these early boyhood years we always got along well, and it was to be so for the rest of our lives. Everything we have done in our business careers has been fifty-fifty. I would say we are also fifty-fifty politically, because he is a Democrat and I am a Republican. I would hasten to add that he is my favorite Democrat.

While we are on this subject, it happens that Averell was a Republican until he voted for Al Smith in 1928. He voted for Al Smith for President and that was when it began for Averell, his career in the Democratic Party. I am a Republican if the Republicans will let me be by putting up good candidates. In other words, I have crossed voting lines. I voted for Al Smith for governor, but not for President. I voted for Lyndon Johnson for President in 1964 against that Arizona fellow.

Both Averell and I were rather awkward when we were young, and we were very congenial. He had—he has always had—a driving desire to excel in whatever he is doing—to be a better man—a better citizen.

Our principal family residence was at Arden, New York, a wondrous place that filled so much of our lives that I shall devote a complete chapter to it as a fitting close to these reminiscences. Finally, in the year before he died, my father bought 1 East Sixty-ninth Street in

7

Manhattan, in which my mother lived until her death much later.

One New York house where we spent the winter when we returned from the Alaska expedition was at 1 East Fifty-fifth Street. This was right opposite what is now the St. Regis Hotel, and the St. Regis was built while we were there. I used to watch it being built when I should have been doing my lessons.

In those days they had horse-drawn dump trucks, and they built a ramp down into the foundation hole, with a small steam donkey engine at the top. They would attach a rope to those wagons in front of the horses, to help pull the wagon up the slope. I remember watching these horses with fascination, straining upward, with a donkey engine going choo-choo-choo. It was quite a sight, compared to the construction methods they use now.

New York City was a wonderful place to be a boy. We would go to Central Park to the Mall, a play area. The kids would all join in and play prisoner's base, cops and robbers, and everything else. We ran about all over the place without any trouble, at least in the parts of the city where I lived.

Later on when I got a little older, I used to roller-skate to school. It was about a mile each way. It seemed like a clean, well-mannered city in which we could roller-skate to school.

I have been asked what we ate in those days. We ate about the same as now but only those growing things that were in season. We used to look forward with great anticipation to things like asparagus, strawberries, peas, lima beans, corn on the cob. Much of this was put in

Mason jars by the cook, but we did not have these delicacies all year round. So they meant much more to us.

I also recall, particularly in summer at Arden when the windows were all open, hearing the cook grind the coffee in an old-fashioned coffee grinder. I remember the delicious smell seeping up through the building when she was making the coffee. We had no instant coffee in those days. Also, on Sunday, I would hear the handyman cranking up the ice cream freezer, as there was only homemade ice cream in the country in those days. There were also lots of good heavy cream and lots of eggs. Shades of cholesterol!

After supper, and before I went to bed, I would spend some time with my father in his study. Damned if I can remember entirely what we did. I remember looking forward to it, very much, as although he was a very stern father, he was a very congenial one. I remember one game we played when we had to tear up paper in little pieces and put them round the room. After I had finished playing the game, I had to pick up all the pieces of paper. He had a special drawer in his desk where he would keep them.

As I grew older, we had wonderful talks together in the study. He was a very short man, approximately five feet five inches, but he never looked short to me. The thing I particularly remember about him is his eyes. He always insisted that I look him straight in the eye whenever I was talking to him. He had no use for people who did not look him in the eye. In fact, I remember he used to say, "That man is all right. He has a firm handshake and he looks you in the eye."

I remember another thing about my father. He was very generous, and would bring me presents once in a

9

while. I wanted to be a fireman. These were the days of horse-drawn fire equipment, and we were living quite close to a firehouse. I used to watch the horses dash out of this building. In fact, I made a collection of toy fire apparatus, and every once in a while my father would bring home a new piece of toy equipment with him. But he would not let me cut the string to open the present. I would have to untie the string and wind it up. Then I would have to take the paper off, fold it tidily, and put both the paper and the string away before he would let me play with the new toy.

My father was also a great one for diaries. He never kept one himself, but he insisted that I keep a diary, one of those line-a-day jobs. He was not very successful, I am afraid, even though he did have a monetary angle. Every day I wrote my diary I would receive a penny. Every day I did not write my diary I would have to pay up two pennies. This way I never got rich.

My father, Edward Henry Harriman, was born in the Episcopal rectory at Hempstead, Long Island, on February 25, 1848. Two years afterward, his father, the Reverend Orlando Harriman, after whom I was to be named, received a call from a mountain parish in California and decided to accept. Reverend Harriman was taken seriously ill at Panama, however, and by the time he reached California, he found that the position had been given to another rector. He wandered about the new state for nearly a year, preaching here and there in pioneer camps and gold-mining towns. He founded Episcopal churches in Stockton and Sacramento, and finally returned to the East in April 1851.

The Harrimans took up their new residence in Jersey City, living in a modest but comfortable home on Hamilton Square. He was a semi-attached curate for several years until, in the early 1860s, he officiated as the rector of a small wooden church named St. John's. He held this office until October 1866.

My father, the third son, was sent off to Trinity School in New York. He continued to live at home, and he walked to the school and back every day via the old Jersey City ferry. At the age of fourteen, my father decided to leave school and go to work.

My father took a job as an office boy in Wall Street at a salary of five dollars a week, in the stock exchange house of D. C. Hayes. At first, his duties were mainly those of a messenger boy. Then he was promoted to the role of "pad-shover." There were no electric tickers to print stock quotations, and the business was conducted by messengers who carried about pads of paper on which current prices and buy and sell offers were scrawled down with pencils. Years later my father commented, "My capital when I began was a pencil and this"—and he tapped the side of his head. Before he was twenty, my father had been promoted to managing clerk.

In the summer of 1870, when he was twenty-two, he borrowed $3,000 from his uncle, Oliver Harriman, a wealthy merchant in the Low, Harriman and Company firm. With this, my father bought a seat on the New York Stock Exchange! Then he opened an office on his own at the corner of Broad Street and Exchange Place.

Four years later, he made a personal profit of approximately $150,000 by selling short in so-called anthracite stocks. He estimated that a speculator was attempting to corner the market and would not make it. My father was proven correct. Eventually, my father concentrated on the development of the railroads, starting in northern New York and later in the western states, but this is a familiar story. I have included these details of his early life because I do not think they are widely known, and also because I think they show interesting glimpses of how he got started.

Through these years, he was making warm personal friends among what were then called social circles—Stuyvesant Fish, James B. Livingston, William Bayard Cutting, Dr. E. L. Trudeau of Saranac Lake and George C. Clark. He became a director of the Travellers Club and a member of the Union and Racquet clubs. He was a keen amateur boxer, and he took lessons from "Larry" Edwards, the brother of the Billy Edwards who was then the light-weight champion. He helped Edwards set up a boxing academy above a candy shop on the corner of Broadway and Twenty-first Street.

One Sunday morning, in one of the first years that we had an automobile, my father decided that we, his boys, should pay a visit to his birthplace at Hempstead, Long Island. So the chauffeur drove my father, Averell and me out to "The Manse," or whatever it was called, the ministerial home of the Reverend Orlando Harriman. It was still there, and it is still there today. When we got back, my mother asked him, "Did you have a nice drive?" He replied, "Yes." She said, "Did the boys like your old homestead?" He replied, "Well, the only one who was impressed was the chauffeur."

I know I was glad to get back to the Sunday papers, with the comics, or "the funnies," as we called them. I was crazy about the funnies; my favorite characters were Old Foxy Grandpa and Buster Brown. But before I was allowed to read the funnies on Sundays, I had to memorize the Collect for the day and recite it to my father.

We were very much like everyone else at that time. We were very much of a family. We did things together, played games together in the evening. My mother was a great one for parlor games, parcheesi and dominoes, also euchre and backgammon. My pride and joy came later on when I was able to persuade the family to play poker.

It seemed I had an awful lot to read at school and at home I enjoyed the books that young boys read—Twain, O. Henry and Henty. I particularly liked it when I could pick out the ones I wanted to read. For instance, at school I read Thackeray's *Henry Esmond*, which was mandatory, and I do not remember a damned word of it.

I went to a young kid's school, at the age of four, called Bovee, which was really meant for young brats. But I used to get a lot of colds. So they sent me down to a school called Pine Lodge at Lakewood, New Jersey, which consisted of six or seven boys.

My father and mother always visited us at Pine Lodge. Once he came down in his automobile and loaded the whole school into it, and drove us all to Atlantic City for the night. We promenaded up and down the boardwalk and enjoyed the sights. I still have a picture of my father's head above the outline of a Teddy bear, which was a popular way of taking photographs at amusement centers.

I remember, in particular, a couple of other incidents at Pine Lodge. Every afternoon we rode around the

13

countryside on horseback. One day my horse tripped over a rut in the sandy road and threw me over his head. The result was a broken collarbone. I was taken home in a horse and buggy and the doctor was sent for from Lakewood, seven miles away. The bone was set but not too adroitly, because my left shoulder, ever since, has been considerably higher than my right. Nothing of consequence except when it comes to fitting me with a coat by the tailor.

Another habit at school involved bathing. There was no inside plumbing for the boys except for the use of the bathtub, but only enough hot water for one tubful. So each evening six boys would take a quick dip in turn and the seventh would linger long enough to use the soap. The boys would rotate so once a week every boy could get good and clean.

Almost immediately after the Russo-Japanese War of 1904-5, my father took the family on a business trip to the Far East. By that time, my father could say that he had a transcontinental transportation system. He also had a line of steamers to ply between the West Coast, Japan and the Philippines. Now, he wanted to negotiate some sort of arrangement to control the Trans-Siberian Railroad so that he could reconstruct a dreadfully inadequate road, after which he would presumably be able to make some kind of arrangement on the Atlantic. His thought was that it would be a great world service, to have a connected first-class round-the-world transportation system.

En route we took a trip through Yellowstone Park. In those days transportation was by stagecoach with a hitch of six horses. I remember the thrill of all the sights, but perhaps most distinctly riding in a cloud of dust when the wind was blowing behind us. The nearest Union Pacific point of entry was a full day's stagecoach ride away. However, my father visualized the increasing use and popularity of the park and within a year a new Union Pacific spur had been built directly to the western entrance of the park. Although it was many years later, this spur was a great help to the Harriman family first to reach the Ranch, of which I will speak later, and then over which to ship our cattle.

During that trip, we actually got to Port Arthur. It was just after the siege there, and I can well remember the sunken hulks of the Russian fleet littered all over the place. It was a little scary because we were told by the Japanese, who were our hosts, that all the mines laid during the war had not yet been recovered. But we went in, and we wandered around the battlefields. There were lots of bodies, not completely buried, with arms and legs sticking up above the ground. We traveled and stayed on a chartered steamer that had brought us across from Japan. I also remember that one member of our party, a doctor, went to join some Japanese at rifle target practice, and outshot them all.

Then we all went over to Peking, and proceeded to the Forbidden City. I have boyish memories of dusty streets, with beggars all over the place. Why I did not die of some horrible disease, I do not know, as I sneaked out of the hotel one day and patronized a seller of dates. I ate the dates, dust and all.

One good thing about the trip—even though the transworld transportation deal was never consummated—was that the Japanese gave my father quite a supply of captured old Russian Napoleon brandy. This we enjoyed for many, many years when I grew up. For many more years than that, I enjoyed telling visiting Japanese businessmen, bankers and others in the United States that I had been in Japan and Manchuria in 1906. This rather startled them, because it was before the days of tourism and right at the start of their growth as a great nation.

One year, my father also took us all to Mexico. My father was, I believe, negotiating with the then dictator, whoever he was, for railroad rights. His work bore some fruit years afterward, when his Southern Pacific built a line down from Tucson, along the west coast of Mexico, toward Mexico City. This was later taken over, however, by the Mexican government.

We also traveled to Europe, and I remember being bored to death by being made to go through all the art museums. I am afraid it did more harm than good, as far as I was concerned, with regard to my appreciation of art.

In fact, my cultural interests were very limited. But I did make a real contribution to the career of one man who became a famous artist. He was a young fellow by the name of James Fraser, who is known to most Americans as the sculptor of the buffalo nickel, as well as of many monuments in Washington and elsewhere.

My sister Mary had become friendly with him, and was very much impressed with his abilities. So she thought she would, as they say, "try it out on the dog," and the dog was me. She got Fraser to come to Arden to sculpt me when I was all of nine years old, and somehow she got me to agree to sit for him throughout what seemed like most of one summer vacation. By the end of the summer, he still had not finished. So I sat for him again through the Christmas holidays, and like any boy of nine, I had changed considerably in appearance during those few months. So he had to make changes, and he did not get finished that holiday either. Not until the following summer did he finish his work—and I consider that I performed a duty to the arts that was good enough to serve for the rest of my life.

Most of my trips with my father were taken on his American railroads, and by the time I was twelve years old, I had visited every state in the Union with the exception of Alabama and North Dakota.

I remember in particular two holidays at Pelican Bay Lodge, a place right on Klamath Lake, in Oregon, renowned for its fishing and for the hunting in the nearby backwoods. To get there, we took the railroad to the end of the line and drove about fifty miles by coach to spend the night in a frontier town called Klamath Falls. The next day, we putted up the lake another twenty-five miles in a naphtha launch to the lodge. We were isolated when we got there, aside from a steamboat that toured with mail and provisions. But my father installed a telegraph line so he could keep in touch with his business affairs. He also kept in touch with my mother and the members of his family who had not gone on the trip. It impressed me after both my parents' deaths to find among the family papers the telegrams my father had sent home every day from Pelican Bay Lodge.

My main recollection of Pelican Lodge was that it was there that I killed my first bear. With the tale of this exploit, I bored my contemporaries for a long time afterward.

On another occasion, we were at Pelican Lodge and a

couple of automobiles came down from Portland to pick us up. When we began to proceed back northward, we were the first automobilists ever to travel across the central part of Oregon from south to north. It was in 1907, I believe, and the reason for the trip was that we were following a survey that was being conducted for a planned railroad from Portland to San Francisco across central Oregon.

The roads, for the most part, were non-existent. There were trails, of a nature, chopped through forests, and if we came to a stream there would probably be no bridge. So we devised a technique in which the first car drove madly at top speed into the stream, to get as far across as possible before the water stalled the engine. We would all get out, push the car the rest of the way, dry off the engine and ourselves and start up. Then the leader would pull the second car across.

One amusing incident occurred when we arrived at a frontier town named Three Sisters, where they were having an annual rodeo. The place was crowded with cowboys and everybody else. There was no room for us at what was laughingly called the hotel. So we put up in kind of an annex. I remember it was dark when we went into our rooms, and there was a bed, a chair and a tin can on the chair. Our family doctor, Dr. Lyle, who was with us on this drive, said, "I'll bet that is bedbug powder." He struck a match and lo and behold, it was bedbug powder.

So we unrolled our sleeping bags and slept on the floor. But we did not get much sleep because the hoopla went on all night long. The cowboys were galloping up and down the street, shooting off their revolvers. This really *was* the Wild West, and I still cannot believe that I really experienced it.

After all, however, those were the days when automobiles were extremely rare almost everywhere, not to mention the wilds of central Oregon. It really was a courtesy, in those days, to slow down when you drove up toward a horse-drawn vehicle, and even to stop until they had gone by. There had been a great many accidents caused by automobiles causing horses to bolt, injuring their drivers and the passengers.

I also remember how the early cops rode not on motorcycles, but on bicycles. More often than not, especially when we were going up hills, the bicycle cops would overtake us, and they would do this quite easily, one way or the other, whenever they wanted to give us a ticket.

And the kids used to run along beside us, in our early automobiles, and yell at us, "Get a horse! Get a horse!" And sometimes we had to, because our automobiles broke down and we had to go and get a horse to tow the things away.

On one of my trips with my father on the railroad, we stopped at a small way station in Texas. A very dignified gentleman in a square derby hat boarded my father's business car, *Arden,* along with a boy just about my age.

The gentlemen talked with one another and the boy and I explored the car. My father was a great one for physical development. He did his chin-ups every morning, and he had a bar attached to the roof of his sleeping quarters. When this other boy saw the bar, he began to chin himself about twenty-five times, and did some acrobatic stunts. I watched with awe and amazement. Everything was fine until I heard my father's voice behind me, "Roland, why can't you do that?"

It was a wonder I ever talked to the boy again, but what should really be said is that the dignified gentleman and his acrobatic son were Judge Robert S. Lovett and his son, Robert A. Lovett. This was the beginning of the association of my father and Judge Lovett in the railroad business. It was Judge Lovett who succeeded my father as the head of the Union Pacific Railroad. And it was also the start of my lasting association with young Bob. We went to different schools, but we were at Yale University together. He became associated with Brown Brothers & Co., private bankers, with which Averell and I merged our companies in 1931. So, since that meeting, Bob Lovett and I have been business partners as well as friendship partners, and in the 1950s we became as one person in the operating of the Union Pacific.

There is a story I would like to tell about him, a story I call "The Ulcer That Won the War." The fellow who produced the ulcer was young Bob Lovett, and the result was that Bob had to stop energetic exercises. But while the rest of us were playing our usual weekend tennis or golf, he refamiliarized himself with a subject he had known a lot about as a naval air pilot in World War I.

These were the 1930s, remember, and Hitler had come into power and was making a lot of unpleasant noises. Sooner or later, Bob thought, we would have to have dealings with him of an unfriendly nature. There was a great hullabaloo in the country that we should build up our fighter force to protect the country from German bombers if and when they flew over the sea to attack us.

Bob Lovett, on the other hand, made up his mind that the answer to German air power was our own super-bombers. On hearing about Bob's theory, Secretary of War Stimson asked Lovett to come to Washington to tell him about it. Stimson asked, "I wish you'd go home and prepare a memorandum of what you have been saying." Lovett said, "Here it is," and pulled a paper out of his pocket. Stimson thought it was so good that he asked Lovett to become Assistant Secretary of War (Air). And remember, it takes four years from the time an airplane goes on the drawing board till the time it is airborne. So the country got bombers when it needed them—and it also got Bob Lovett.

From then on, Bob was so valuable the government would not let him go. He was Assistant Secretary of Defense, Assistant Secretary of State, Deputy Secretary of Defense and, finally, Secretary of Defense in the Truman administration. After all this, with his sense of humor still intact, Bob returned to Brown Brothers Harriman.

I remember another occasion when my father took me with him on one of his business trips. We went down to Washington, D.C. I was just a little brat, but he had to give some testimony to the Interstate Commerce Commission and he took me along. I remember his saying that the Union Pacific had just built several all-steel boxcars. This was the first steel freight equipment that had ever been built.

By now I was well aware, of course, that my father had become head of the Union Pacific in 1898. He died in 1909, so almost everything he did was accomplished in eleven years. He bought control, or at least the Union Pacific bought control, of the Southern Pacific during that period without having to get anybody's permission.

First of all, he raised a lot of money through sales of securities, preferred stock, bonds and common stock to rebuild the Union Pacific, without anybody's permission and without having to ask anybody's permission. He obtained control of his large interests in other railroads also without having to ask anybody's permission, at least at the governmental end of things. It was fantastic what he accomplished in eleven years.

What brought this home to me quite recently was that eleven years ago the modern Union Pacific attempted to acquire the Chicago, Rock Island and Pacific Railroad. Governmental permission has not yet been granted, and the answer is nowhere near in sight. This is just one of the differences between doing business now and the way things were seventy years ago.

I did mention this not long ago to a recent head of the Interstate Commerce Commission, who replied, "Well, if all the people doing business at the turn of the century had been like your father, there would have been no need for the Interstate Commerce Commission." It is the old story: the crooks are the ones who require controls, and the innocent suffer along with them.

On one such trip to Washington, I remember my father taking me with him to the White House to meet President Theodore Roosevelt. In those days, or so it seemed, you just strolled in and called on the President. There was no fuss and no fury.

At that time, Teddy and my father were very good friends. Then they had their famous falling out. Teddy did not help after that by calling my father a "malefactor of great wealth." I cannot remember any exact event that created the friction between Roosevelt and my father. I think it was a general philosophical problem. Teddy made a great name for himself for trust busting, wielding the big stick in all the cartoons of the day, and I think my father rather resented this. He thought that people of good will and good manners and good ethics should be left alone by the government. He was just as anxious to develop the country as Teddy was.

This was why my father had spent all his time and energy building the western railroads, to help develop the western states. He certainly accomplished that purpose. Without the western railroads, of which the Union Pacific was one, the West might still be a frontier.

Right up until World War II, the major flow of goods and commodities had always been from the East to the West, with the exception of the great agricultural products. During the war, this changed, and afterward shipments from the West exceeded those from the East. The West is now not only an agricultural region, very clearly, but is a capital goods producer and an expanding market for all goods and services. It was my father's ambition to bring the country into a more even balance, just as it was Teddy Roosevelt's. I wish they had both been able to live to see it fulfilled.

At any rate, our families did not let this unpleasantness intrude unduly. Archie Roosevelt attended Groton with me, and he had the desk next to me, and we were good friends. Ethel Roosevelt was a good friend of my sister Carol.

On the steamer on the return trip from Japan our party

was joined by Alice Roosevelt, who was returning from a trip to the Philippines. My father invited the President's daughter to accompany us on a special train headed east. My father liked speed, and, as usual, he was in a hurry, and the speed of the train reached such proportions that it attracted the attention of station watchers and some of the journalists. Almost as soon as the train was under way, the newspapers were commenting about its dangerous speed.

The result was that my father received a telegram in mid-journey from President Roosevelt. It read: PLEASE TAKE CARE OF THE SAFETY OF MY DAUGHTER ON YOUR TRAIN. In reply, my father wired the President of the United States: YOU RUN THE COUNTRY. I'LL RUN THE RAILROAD.

Sometimes it did seem unnecessary and unfair when Teddy Roosevelt termed my father "an enemy of the republic," but these were the days when businessmen were fair game. I still keep on the wall of my office a cartoon by McCutcheon of the Chicago *Tribune* depicting my father's so-called plans for reorganizing all the railroads of the country. It shows my father sitting behind his desk telling the magnate Jay Gould, "Here, Gould, take this dictation." On his desk is a motto, "I hope a lion bites him." A sanitation man who looks like J. Pierpont Morgan, with a label "Morgan," is saying to my father, "Shall I wash the windows today?"

I also keep a photograph of my father at his rolltop desk, his coat and hat slung over the side of it. He did not have a hatrack. He is sitting in a plain, ordinary wicker chair, with an old-fashioned telephone standing at his left hand. The thing that tickles me the most about the photograph is that one of the drawers even has a drawer handle missing. This is all very different from modern decor.

I have many other reminiscences, somewhat apropos in this present day, when everybody seems to be looking at one another to determine whether or not they are crooks. Anyway, I think it was in 1904 that the Union Pacific jumped its dividend from four dollars a share to eight dollars a share, all at once, at a meeting of the Board of Directors. This created quite an uproar and there was much suspicion about inside information. Some governmental group investigated, and one of the witnesses was my father.

As I recall, one of the pertinent questions asked was, "Did you buy any stock in anticipation of the jump in the dividend?" My father replied, "I most certainly did." Well, they thought they had him. They asked, "When, and at what price?" He said, "Most of it in 1896 at prices of three to seven dollars a share."

As I grew older, I was to become increasingly concerned about these attacks on my father's reputation. These were continued unabated after his death. I hope, in fact, that these reminiscences will help restore the perspectives of a great man. I am also aware that I have talked more, so far, about my father than about my mother. This will be rectified in the section of the reminiscences I have planned for Arden, where my fondly cherished memories of my mother flower to this day.

CHAPTER II: GROWING UP

At the age of eleven, in 1907, I went to Groton. I was a year younger than my classmates, and I had a terrible struggle to keep up. In fact, the headmaster suggested, at one time, that I repeat a year. My father would have none of it, and I was expected to prove that my father was right.

They were happy days at Groton, however. I was in the lower third of the form scholastically, to start with. Fortunately, by my fifth- and six-form years, I was up in the upper third. I never liked Greek, but the other subjects I came to like pretty well. History was my favorite subject. Oh yes, French, that was another story. French I despised. But I rocked along pretty well through the Groton years, all things considered.

There had been two things lacking at the school when Averell, who preceded me by four years, and I went there. One was an athletic director, and the other was a tutor who would be available to help boys who needed it, boys like me. Fortunately, my father made arrangements to help supply these two needs, and I am deeply grateful to Mr. Andrews, the tutor, a very fine gentleman indeed. My father also kept a very close watch on my progress. Everybody had to write a letter home on Sundays, and at my father's and mother's demand, I also wrote them a postcard every night. Once a week our marks came out, and I had to send them too.

My parents thus kept pretty good tabs on me at Groton, as to whether I was still floundering or making progress, and as far as I was concerned, I had better make progress. I was never punished if I did not, or anything like that. But I could tell during holiday periods whether my name was welcome at home or not, in the scholastic sense. In any event, things went well at Groton, as I have said.

I used to love the library up there, and I used to spend hours there on Sundays with my nose buried in—of all things—old copies of *Punch,* the British humor magazine. I methodically went back through old issues, and in those days *Punch* was the best history textbook I had ever come across. There were not only jokes that made the period come alive, but there was real history contained in the articles and the cartoons. There was one I remember in particular of Kaiser Wilhelm II of Germany kicking Bismarck out, dated 1890, I think, entitled "Dropping the Pilot." Bismarck was shown walking down the companion way, dignified and old. The Kaiser, with his spiky moustache, was leaning on the rail surveying the scene with a look of contempt. That cartoon was prophetic, showing what was happening to Germany in those days long before World War I.

History was my favorite all through Groton. I like to know where we have gone before. And I must say that I had a criticism to make of history teachers who made us

28

learn all the names and dates of the French and English kings while neglecting to tell us that, one hundred years before the Pilgrim fathers landed in Massachusetts, the Spaniards were in California. Later I could not understand this. It was only in my adult life that I really found out about the history of the North American continent. We had been told in an offhand way about Cortez's attack on Mexico, but that was all. They talked about the English colonies but not about Spain.

At Groton I also participated in sports. I was kind of an awkward cuss until I got to rowing. I rowed on the crew for the last two years, mainly thanks to the coaching I received from Jim Ten Eyck, as we will learn later. I do remember, however, that football caused me a little trouble. Due to my frequent trips out West, I had acquired some of the western language, cowboy expletives, if you like. And I remember one time, when I was captain of the Second Monadnocks, an interscholastic club, I cussed out one of the players on my team. After the game was over, the master in charge told me, "I'm sorry, but I'll have to report you to the rector for profanity." I replied, "Golly, what did I say?" The master was mute.

I was reprimanded by the rector, and my punishment perhaps made a liar out of me. For thirty days, whenever I said good night to the rector, I had to say, "Mr. Peabody, I did not swear today." The Mr. Peabody, incidentally, was the awe-inspiring Endicott Peabody himself. But such were my instinctive habits I could not accurately recall whether I had sworn that day or not.

At Groton, religious life was taken for granted. Church was the thing to do. We went to church on Sundays, compulsory daily morning chapel and Sunday chapel. Actually, they did not call it compulsory at Groton. It was just the thing to do.

One real contribution that my religious education made to me was that it gave me a nickname. In my first-form year, the rector held a class named Sacred Studies every Monday, at which we learned, among other things, the Christian calendar, Epiphany, Lent and so on. One time he was away, and there was a rascal of a master sitting in for whom nobody had much respect. When we got to the place of Easter on the calendar I stuck up my hand and asked, "Why do we have rabbits at Easter?" Well, this man considered my question irreligious, or thought I was just being sassy, because he stuck me with the heaviest punishment he could, six black marks.

From that time on, I was called "Bunny." I liked Bunny much better than my old nickname, which had been "Rolly." And ever since then, I have liked to ask people if they know why we have rabbits at Easter, and nobody ever knows.

After my father died in 1909, my mother very intelligently decided that I should have $100 a year for every year of my age, as an allowance. But if this sounds like a lot, I had to pay my school tuition out of it. I had to pay for all my books, athletic equipment, clothes and everything except travel and medical expenses. I would usually end up every year with about ten dollars in the bank. It was close going.

At that time, tuition at Groton ran to less than $1,000 —much less than now. But having to pay my own school bills did help teach me how to handle money, how to save money and how to spend it only on the things I really needed or wanted. I must say I found it easy to handle my personal finances, and as we grew older, both Averell and I were given substantial sums to handle, which was another intelligent step on my mother's part. Yet I still remember the early days at Groton because, on our arrival, the boys had to turn in all their money over one dollar, so they could not run away from school, I guess. Then we were given twenty-five cents a week, ten cents of which had to go into the plate at Sunday chapel, and that left fifteen cents for the candy shop when we went down to the village.

We used to trek nearly two miles to the village, each way, on Saturdays, to get an ice cream soda—an energetic way to satisfy a sweet tooth.

I rather think walking is an excellent element in education and today I really do object to school bussing, not bussing to create racial equality, but bussing as transportation that makes it impossible for the kids to walk. When they centralized the schools, making transportation by busses and automobile necessary, the kids lost an awful lot in physical and character development. Nowadays, people are not satisfied even to have kids assembled every five or six blocks to be picked up. They want to be picked up at every damned block. This creates a terrible disturbance for other users of the roads, and a loss of opportunity for the kids.

At Groton I sang in the choir, God knows why, because I have no ear for music. I cannot keep a tune, but for some reason the choir intrigued me. I even took singing lessons, as a result of which I was allowed to become at least a semi-silent member of the choir.

One of the most important things for me at Groton,

however, was the printing press. This I loved. There was a master at Groton who was tops, in my opinion, a man named Mather Abbott. For some reason or other, I never knew quite why, he decided it would be a good thing for the boys to learn a trade. He hit on printing. So he started in a very small way, with a little foot press, and just one font of type, in a small room. This fascinated me, as I always loved to do things with my hands. And by the time I graduated, the printing operation was taking up a large part of the cellar of the schoolhouse. We had a power press, a power typesetting machine, a folder and cutter and all the rest, and we published the weekly newspaper and the monthly paper *The Grotonian*. We set type, printed, cut, folded and everything else. This was a real education, and it kept my hands dirty the whole time I was at Groton. It is hard to get rid of printer's ink.

Then, when automobiles really began to come along in large numbers, I became a sort of amateur mechanic during holiday periods. Automobiles fascinated me. In those early days, it seemed to me that you could fix automobiles with a screwdriver and a hairpin. I was just about able to take them apart, and put them back together again, without too many spare parts being left out. Nowadays, by contrast, everything about automobiles is too complicated. Not even the modern mechanics know how to fix the modern automobiles.

In the first place, I was brought up while we were in the horse and buggy age. Ours was essentially a horse family. There was nothing but horses. We had horses to drive and horses to ride. All the other members of the family were ardent horsemen, and they insisted upon my being one. Initially I hated the horse, and then, while I was growing up a bit, the automobile began to come into more popular use. So I joined the crowd that liked automobiles, while the family gradually converted to automobiles for distance transportation.

I remember the consternation of the family when we happened to be in Newport, Rhode Island, and we visited the famous Vanderbilt stables. Mr. Vanderbilt showed us around with great pride. Then he turned to me and said, "Roland, do you like horses?" I replied, "I'd rather have an automobile." I had managed in this gentleman's eyes to insult the whole family.

My ambition was to have an automobile of my own, and when I was about fifteen, my mother consented, provided that I made a good record at school. And what I got that summer was one of the original Hupmobiles. In those days, there were all kinds and characters of automobiles, with many more and different makes than there are now. My Hupmobile was a little two-seater, two-speed job, with just about three-dog power. I had a wonderful time with it, traveling all the back roads, though my mother had the chauffeur go with me. This was even more fun, as the chauffeur had once been a mechanic for the legendary racing driver Barney Oldfield, and he taught me the fundamentals of good, safe driving techniques which have stood me well to this day.

Then I got my second car several years later, a Mercer Raceabout. This was supposed to be very racy, but to compare it to modern automobiles, I would have to tell another story. One Sunday, when I was down from college, I took our family doctor, Dr. Lyle, out to Long Island to the Vanderbilt Speedway. They had a measured

33

mile and, three times, I tore down that measured mile. The highest speed I attained was 70 mph. Well, I remember that Barney Oldfield used to win his races not much earlier at an average speed of say 60 mph, which is about start-up speed for modern cars today.

As time passed, however, I did take to horses, and never liked anything better. I became intensely interested in trotting horses, and this is not just another story. It is another chapter.

At first I had made up my mind that I wanted to go to Princeton. Then I made up my mind it would be Harvard. So I finally ended up at Yale. I went there in the fall of 1913, and that made me a freshman member of the Class of 1917.

Yale did more than give me a modicum of a good education. It gave me an interest in outside affairs and taught me how to conduct myself in a grown-up world as well as how to pick and choose men as friends and associates. I think Yale did a good job, and I think it is too bad that so many graduates of the universities are now blaming the colleges for the mess that education is in.

I remember in the 1960s we were all bewailing the riots that were taking place on campus. Well, looking further back, doggone it, every spring at Yale we had a riot, though not of the caliber of the modern riots. But something would always happen, and we decided it was either right or wrong, and we yelled at everybody to come out in the streets, and we paraded around and made a great deal of racket, and that was about the extent of it.

Except for one evening when we ended up, somehow,

outside the house of the secretary of the university, a man by the name of Phelps Stokes. He had a rather saturnine face, with a goatee beard and a moustache, and we felt like yelling and shouting outside his house.

Stokes finally stuck his head out of a window. It was draped in—believe it or not—an old nineteenth-century nightcap! This was too much, but we hushed up when he began to address us. He said, "Gentlemen, I cannot thank you enough for coming to see me off for my trip to Europe." We did not even know he was going, but that was how that riot ended.

I remember also that there was a lot of excitement at Yale about the movies, which were just coming into fashion. I am afraid I spent a lot of my time, and a lot of my friends spent more time, than we all should have at the movies instead of studying. I was probably an expert on the movies. *The Perils of Pauline* was a famous serial adventure story. Pearl White was the star, and in my book she still is a star. There were also the Keystone Cops.

The Perils of Pauline would be played in a movie theater converted out of two or three small, smelly stores in New Haven. There would be a projector upstairs and the whole place would probably hold about one hundred people. A pianist would sit banging away in front; we all used to love the pianist, too. She would follow the script very well. When the cavalry came on, she would go "Boop! Boop! Boop!"

Oh sure, we all cheered. And then there was none of this automatic motion picture equipment. When they came to the end of a reel, it would be "One moment, please," and they would change to another reel. This was also received very enthusiastically by the students.

35

Academically, I took economics and history as majors. My grades were medium, neither good nor bad. There was nothing to write home about my grades. Professor Mims was the history teacher who impressed me the most.

Originally, I had intended to go into the railroading business when I got out of college, so I also took courses I thought would help me. In my senior year, I signed up for a course on railroading. And that was where Yale really double-crossed me. Just before the senior year arrived, they fired the professor that gave the course. I inquired why. And do you know why? This professor lived out in the country, and before he came into class, he used to clean out his barn. He used to come to the university smelling of manure, and that was the reason for firing him.

Another thing happened to me while I was at Yale. My horse fell while fox hunting and I broke my neck—and lived. I had to go around in a plaster cast from my neck to my hips for all of one term. Perhaps this even robbed the world of a great biologist. I had signed up for a course in biology, but we had to look down through microscopes to look at the bugs. Well, with this plaster cast around me, I could not look down through any microscope. But no lasting damage was done.

Rowing I really enjoyed, and thereby hangs many a tale concerning my brother and me. My father had been a physical fitness enthusiast, as I have said, and one summer he had convinced the head coach of the Syracuse University crew, a man by the name of Jim Ten Eyck, to spend six weeks at Arden with Averell and me to teach us how to row. For six weeks we went through regular training sessions. Up before breakfast, row in a barge, a two-oared barge, then a row in single sculls, morning and afternoon. We became oarsmen, pretty good ones, if I say it myself.

Unfortunately, when Averell was about seventeen, at Groton, and he was rowing on the crew, the doctors thought they discovered a heart murmur. They made him stop rowing. When Averell went on to Yale, he knew the techniques backward and forward and in his senior year he was appointed head coach of the Yale crew.

Averell took a trip to England to see how they rowed over there. He wondered whether the Yale crew should convert to the English stroke, together with the tholepins and everything else. He persuaded three of the top English oarsmen to come back to the United States to help teach the Yale crew how to row that stroke. The results were excellent.

One of my recollections of the Englishmen is that they invited me to return with them to attend the Henley regatta. This turned out to be quite a historic trip which had nothing to do with rowing. While in this country, the Englishmen had become rather enamored of the American martini. In those days, the English had no martinis. They had gin and bitters.

Well, the afternoon we arrived in London, we all scattered out around the London shopping district to find a cocktail shaker. At that time, martinis were shaken, not stirred. Finally we all ended up at the house we were all staying in as guests and compared results. Four of us had been unsuccessful. The fifth had found just one shaker in all of London at Selfridge's, a huge department store that happened to be American-owned.

So I can say I was one of the five people who introduced martinis into England.

My athletic activity at Yale was concentrated on rowing and I have very fond memories of it, although I only once had the thrill of seeing the rival crew behind us as we crossed the finish line. In freshman year, I rowed number five position on the class's first boat. Sophomore year was the period I broke my neck, followed by an appendicitis operation. So I was asked to coach our class crew, which became champion of Yale but was beaten by Harvard. Then, along with another semi-cripple, I was taken along as substitute for the varsity crew to Gales Ferry, the scene of the preparation for the all-important Harvard race. Fortunately, the members of both the first and second boats beat Harvard handily.

In my junior year, I remained hale and hearty and rowed on the varsity crew all season, starting as stroke and winding up as bow. Our season was not a success. The spring of senior year saw our country's entry into World War I so our rowing season was curtailed.

I had a fine lot of classmates. Knight Woolley, who has been one of my closest personal and business friends, was one of my classmates. So was Ellery James, who was also to become one of my closest associates. Prescott Bush of Connecticut, a business and personal partner as well as a United States senator, was a classmate. Bob Lovett, that acrobatic young friend of mine, was a class behind.

We had a good run of young people in Yale 1917 who became businessmen, professors, artists and even a Nobel Prize winner in medicine. They must have been a pretty hardy lot, because quite a few of them are still living.

One of my Yale memories is spectacular, to say the

least. I had blown myself to a parlor car seat en route to New Haven and another passenger had bought the same seat. I had gotten there first and then the other man was standing there, looking down at me. It was none other than William Howard Taft, former President of the United States, who was doing a stint as a professor at Yale. The dilemma was resolved when the conductor got him another seat.

Taft was a great baseball fan at that time, and he used to go to all the college baseball games. He would always buy two seats so there would be enough room for his massive girth. One time, an usher took him to his seat at the game and began to stammer and blush. Taft asked, "What's the matter, young man, what's the matter?" The man said, "Sir, the two seats are on opposite sides of the aisle."

Basically, I had congenial friends and a good life at Yale. I worked hard. Yale was close enough to New York to get down to on Saturday, and get back from in time to go to church on a Sunday morning. Perhaps this was the last of the easy life at Yale, however, because 1917 was the year in which all hell broke out. In fact, we never had a full graduation of our class. All our people were here and there in the armed forces. But I am moving ahead perhaps a little too fast, and there is more of Yale to tell.

One thing I remember about my mother is how when we began to go out to parties and dances at night, she always asked us to come in and say good night to her no matter what time we got in. Sometimes there would be as many as three of us going out—my unmarried sister, my brother and myself. She must have had rather restless nights, because we would all have to come in and say good night to her. We really loved doing this, and thought it was a nice thing to do. And I am convinced, with the way life was then, that she was not checking up on us, but wanted to know merely that we had arrived safely home.

In those days, there was never much drinking at social affairs. Cocktails were never served at the house. We had wine, but not hard liquor. At dances champagne would be served in small quantities at supper for the men, but most of the girls drank milk. These must have been quite inexpensive parties to run, compared to the parties today. In fact, I often think that it was only after Prohibition came in that people began to drink heavily.

I remember one time my mother was shocked and horrified because one of my elder sister's friends boarded the family yacht and demanded cocktails. She told him no gentleman drank cocktails at that time in the afternoon and nobody would ever demand cocktails without first being asked.

But people used to gorge themselves on food at public functions in those days. The menus I saw would go on and on forever. Then there would be after-dinner speakers. There were no loudspeakers in those days, and the after-dinner speakers had to rely on their unaided voices. Some of them, as a result, developed fine oratorical voices and were in great demand.

It must have been awful to have to listen to all this shouting and flourishing, full of food, listening to it going on and on. I am glad that in this respect our lives have changed.

On the debutante circuit in those days, the girls "came out," approximately at the age of eighteen. There would also be some dances for younger girls, which were very popular with the schoolboys, and then the debutantes would come out at the time their boy friends were in college.

I remember how some hosts used to make names for their families—or try to—by the extravagance of their girl's coming out party. I remember one party in which there were special cars to and from Boston and New Haven and Princeton to bring the college boys to the affair. I did not happen to go, but my friends returned goggle-eyed from the experience, telling me about a trick they had played on a classmate. There was quite an exhibition of jewels at this party, and a large number of private detectives were roaming around. During supper, my friends slipped some pieces of silver flatware into our classmate's pocket, and afterward, as he rushed out from the stag line to pick up some girl, they tripped him and down he went, silver spewing all over the floor around him. The detectives were on him in a flash.

The dances used to be personal affairs, with personal friends there, and everybody had a good time. I remember we even used to have plenty of room on the dance floor to dance in, and only later did the whole thing get into mass production. Soon the ballrooms were too crowded, and we would be lucky if we could dance at all.

It was in my time that they started the phenomenon known as the stag line. There were dance cards at first. They used to have a girl's boy friend, or brother, or somebody fill out the dance cards with suitable partners in advance. This led from one extreme to the other, to the stag line. The stags would simply dash out from the line to cut in on a couple. If a girl was popular, she might be able to get about three steps with a single partner. If she was unpopular, she might be stuck with one partner far too long.

Another feature of social life was that the girls had to have chaperones. They could not be brought to the dance by their boy friends. Also, some families began to use social secretaries. These people would compile lists of eligible young men at Harvard, Yale and Princeton and elsewhere. We would sometimes get invitations from people we had never heard of. Some of our classmates were rude enough not to acknowledge or answer these invitations, and then, at the last minute, turn up.

But at least we did have wonderful music and we did have great dances. We had a lot of waltzes, and we had ragtime, two-steps and so on. The tango started at that time, but I was never any good at that one. Waltzes were my favorite. We really danced! We did not just stand in the middle of the floor and wiggle our hips.

It was fun.

The most remarkable summer I had during Yale days was the summer of 1915. My mother generously let me take the family yacht *Sultana* with a group of friends—male friends—around through the newly completed Panama Canal to San Francisco. The *Sultana* was an old-timer my father had bought in 1904 or 1905. She was a coal-burner, with a top speed of only eight knots, but she was very comfortable. Previously, we had used her mostly for cruising up and down Long Island Sound and the coast of Maine, but now we were off to one of San Francisco's periodic World's Fairs.

This was between my sophomore and junior year at

Yale, and most of the passengers were classmates. Dr. Lyle was also on board, and so was Mather Abbott, who had been one of my teachers at Groton. He had moved on to Yale, and would later go to Lawrenceville as headmaster. I imagine my mother sent him along as a balance wheel for the rest of us.

We had a glorious six weeks. We stopped at Jacksonville and Havana, and had a wild time in Jamaica. We landed on the north coast of Jamaica, at a little village called Port Antonio. We were told the mountainous interior of the island was very beautiful, so we motored across to Kingston.

Remember, this was 1915, and we were able just to collect a couple of broken-down old cars to take us across the mountains. One of them, a Ford, had brake trouble running down the hills. The driver braked the thing by catching hold of tree branches as we rolled down. Finally, this car ran into the bank at the side of the road, and I still do not know how we all made it to Kingston.

We went through the Panama Canal, which was a magnificent sight, even though there was nothing untoward about it. Then we put into the bay at Acapulco on the west coast of Mexico for coal. Acapulco is now a very posh resort, of course, but when we landed there was nothing other than a small town built on a peninsula projecting into the harbor. There was a mule trail over the mountains and one telegraph line to civilization.

At this time, Mexico was in the throes of recurrent revolutions, and one of the key places in town was an old fort. Whenever the inmates of the fort got bored with one another, or so we were told, they chose up sides. One side stayed inside the fort, and the other side got out of the fort, and tried to get back in again. At least, that was what it sounded like when we were there. There was desultory popping of guns and when we asked the American consul about it, he said, "Yes, they're just having a good time."

The consul added that the people inside the fort ought to have no trouble winning, because they had some artillery in there. It turned out they did have artillery, but it would not work. They had a three-inch field gun they had neglected to take care of, and one of the shells had gotten jammed in the breech. The people in the fort asked the captain of a visiting American warship for help in fixing the fieldpiece. The captain took one look at the filth and rust of the gun, and said, "The first thing you've got to do is to clean it up, and I'll come back, and perhaps we can do something about it." He came back the next day and yes, they had cleaned it up, but with gray paint, both inside and out.

Well, the Mexican coal was about as good as their gunnery, and we had trouble propelling the *Sultana* to San Diego. But there was no more excitement, and we made it the rest of the way to San Francisco without incident. It was an unforgettable vacation.

When World War I broke out, my mother gave the *Sultana* to the United States Navy, and the old ship was pressed into service as, of all things, a submarine chaser. The *Sultana* did in fact chase one U-boat and dropped a depth charge. She was so slow she hardly got out of the way of the explosion herself, and she certainly did not sink the submarine. And the Navy did more damage than they should have, because they used the cabins for coal bunkers.

When the *Sultana* was returned to us after the war, there seemed nothing else to do but get rid of her. We sold her to a motion picture company, which used her as a location for their production. But I am sorry to relate that my final sight of the *Sultana* was a sad one indeed. There she lay, on a mudbank in Los Angeles Harbor, abandoned.

A vacation trip with greater significance in my life had meanwhile been taken by Bob Lovett. He had gone to Europe with his family one summer, and while his parents were doing whatever they were doing, Bob hired a motorcycle and went off to Switzerland. About five miles out of St. Moritz he skidded and dumped himself in freshly spread tar. Bob was in a terrible mess.

Bob then drove on to the hotel in St. Moritz and there he was taken in tow by an American named Dr. Harold H. Fries. Dr. Fries took charge of Bob and got his suit cleaned up. And, of course, he introduced Bob to his daughter Gladys. So that was where Bob met Gladys, and that autumn Bob introduced me to Gladys, and about six months after that, Gladys and I were engaged. We were engaged two years before we were married in 1917. So I give Bob the credit or the blame, whatever way you want to look at it.

Not that Bob was himself interested in Gladys Fries. He already had his eye on the girl he would eventually marry. This was Adele Brown, the daughter of James Brown, of the Brown Brothers firm. She was a great friend of all of us, and still is. We still kid Bob about marrying the boss's daughter, and about how he became a partner.

Harold Fries was born in New York, of a family that

had come across from Germany. He had two principal interests. One was chemistry. He was a manufacturing chemist, and that was one reason he went to Europe every year, with his family, to maintain his chemical relationships with people on the other side. His other interest was in a torsion balance company which made very fine weighing scales for pharmacies and scientific laboratories. I remember he told me some time before he died, "Roland, when I die, get rid of the chemical business as quickly as you can. There is no money in chemicals. There is only money in agreements. But hang on to the balance company. There is a little gold mine." And he was right.

Dr. Fries was very happily married to Catherine Cahill, a girl from Dayton, Ohio, and Gladys was their only child. They were very attractive people, and Dr. Fries used to love to surround himself with young people. Everybody called him "Dada." He lived on West Fifty-ninth Street in an old-fashioned apartment house, an outgoing, blustering man, with a great mate, charming, retiring, sweet, with a very definite mind of her own.

I remember another thing about the Fries family. He had been interested at one time in a lumber company in the South. When the lumber was about used up, he took over the area and maintained it as a quail-shooting preserve. There they retained an old southern atmosphere, with a simple but old and lovely mansion, brought up to date. The older blacks on the place had been slaves. Their children were taught by Mrs. Fries how to be house servants and they were a credit to everybody concerned. There was good quail shooting down there, too.

So that was a very happy family, the Frieses, and on April 12, 1917, a very happy, lovely girl became my wife.

46

She had graduated from Spence the year before and was active in the Junior League in New York City. She was not a social butterfly in any way at all, but she had oodles of friends, and she traveled with them, and house-partied and weekended. During the week she worked very seriously indeed at the Junior League, and she used to manage the performances of amateur theatricals the Junior League put on to raise a great deal of money. She was a great manager—still is. She took after her father.

I met her in Tuxedo Park, New York, at a party given by mutual friends. It was just a big party and she knew lots of my friends. There was no spark between us that first evening, nothing like love at first sight. We were congenial, and we became friends, and so on and so forth, and finally we suddenly realized that we wanted to marry one another.

Parenthetically, I do not understand why young men at school these days are so anxious to have co-educational education. In my day, there would come the holidays, and we would fuss the girls, have a great time with them, and then we would go back to school and be glad to get rid of them for a while, to get them out of our hair. Now they seem to want to commingle at an early age. It is a funny thing, or so they tell me at the Boys Club in New York, that the boys there are becoming interested in girls at least two years earlier than they used to. Maybe there has been a physiological change.

There was one wonderful evening, after we were married, when we were still being asked to some of the debutante parties. There was one at the old Ritz Hotel, a particularly attractive place, and we had gone to the theater first. When we arrived, all the other guests had gone into supper, and suddenly the band came back into the ballroom ahead of time. The leader was an old friend of ours, and he knew how much Gladys and I loved to waltz. So he struck up a waltz and for about fifteen minutes we danced the waltz alone without another soul in the ballroom. This still stands out in my mind. It was a delightful evening.

So I had grown up to be a railroad man. Of course, every kid in those days wanted to be a railroad engineer, but I wanted to be in the business because I had seen it. I knew what it was about. I had consorted with railroad men, men who were associates of my father's, and it was a great business. It had been my intention to start in Portland, Oregon. But then Kaiser Bill upset all these well-laid plans and everything was turned upside down.

Of course, we had not been rocking along at Yale oblivious to the world situation. There had been the Mexican scare, with Pancho Villa's raids on the New Mexico villages, and of course the massive conflict was raging in Europe. Military preparedness had become a popular subject in our country, and a lot of my friends joined what was then the equivalent of the ROTC.

Even after we entered World War I, there was much thought that America would send supplies and ammunition to the Allies but would somehow stay out of direct fighting. As I was mechanically minded, I applied to the Army Ordnance Department for a commission, and was accepted. I was sent to inspect plants making ordnance of all kinds.

On one of these missions, in Lowell, Massachusetts, I

caught pneumonia, and it soon seemed obvious that I would take some time getting over it. There were no nurses available at that time and Gladys nursed me completely. By the following September, in the second year of the war, I was well enough to be back on the inspection round, and I was inspecting a Canadian outfit in Toronto. Then I came down with a virulent attack of influenza. This did not help the pneumonia.

By this time I had applied for the artillery so that I could get into the fighting, but the combination of pneumonia and influenza was too much. At that point, I was told I had incipient tuberculosis and that I was seriously ill. I was still sick in Toronto when the Armistice was signed, and World War I was over.

In December 1918 I was shipped off to Santa Barbara, California, with doctor's orders to stay for a year, and with almost everybody's expectation that I would be forced to remain in that equable climate for the rest of my life.

In the following February, our first child was born, a girl, Betty. Gladys' family had been disturbed about her having a child in a frontier town like Santa Barbara, and so had arranged for a specialist from Los Angeles to deliver the baby. Events moved too rapidly, however, and the weather was inclement—in fact, it was a terrible night —and the baby was delivered in Santa Barbara by the general practitioner. There was no trouble at all. About three hours too late, the specialist arrived from Los Angeles to find the baby sound asleep. This did not deter him from sending us a big bill.

After about four or five months, I fooled my friends by feeling a lot better. I thought I ought to have something to do, so I decided to buy what they called a ranch, but which we in the East would call a farm. We narrowed down to two choices. One was a very attractive ranch located on the coast to the west of Santa Barbara. The other was in the foothills. On my doctor's advice, I bought the one in the foothills, so as to avoid the fogs that sometimes enveloped the coast. When we closed the deal, the owner brought out a bottle of wine to seal our signatures. It was pretty good wine, but we later found out he and his wife had made it by tramping their own grapes in a barrel. We had no ill effects.

We worked the ranch ourselves, with the help of a farmer, and this was a lot of fun as well as useful therapy. I was all for tearing up the wine grapes, but my wife prudently stopped me, and this was fortunate because the grapes became our most profitable crop. Before Prohibition, wine grapes sold for two dollars a ton. After Prohibition, the going rate was something like fifty dollars a ton. We never regretted buying the place, although we did have difficulty with water.

But what about the ranch we did not buy, the one along the coast? Three or four years after we passed it by, a major oil strike was made on that property. And just to wind up that story, I happened to develop a friendship many years after that with Charlie Jones, then the president of Richfield Oil and subsequently a partner in our ranch in Idaho. I was telling Charlie the story about the ranch in Santa Barbara which we did not buy when he seemed suddenly interested. He asked me, "Do you know who it was who struck that oil?" I said, "I haven't the slightest idea." And Charlie said, "I did." He had been the twenty-two-year-old geologist who made the strike.

50

So there we were in Santa Barbara, at the age of twenty-three, an age at which all of the major professional decisions in life ought to be well in hand. I did not know what was going to happen. I rode with the punches. I was not depressed. I had a lovely wife, a tiny but comfortable home and a new baby. I just did not believe the doctors. I thought I was going to snap out of it, and fortunately I was right because eleven months later my doctor said I was fit to go back East if I wanted to.

I was glad to go back East, if only because one of the favorite pursuits of Santa Barbara was beach picnics. One thing I hate is a picnic on the beach, and the one trouble with Santa Barbara was that between April and November there was sure to be no rain!

So we came home. For years I had to do more or less what the doctor said, and did not get overtired. I had to be careful, and it was ten to twelve years before I finally shook off the effects of that illness.

CHAPTER III: BOATS, BUGS, BRIDGES AND BOYS

A couple of years ago, a young man studying management at a business school in California wrote me, and asked me three questions. He was writing his final paper and wanted to incorporate my answers in it. He asked, firstly: to what did I owe my success in gaining my present positions; secondly, what did I look for in a successor I would choose to replace me; and thirdly, what were the real guts of management as I saw it.

Well, I found this very intriguing, and after a lot of thought, I wrote the young man that three words suffice to answer all three questions. The virtues I looked for were knowledge, enthusiasm and common sense.

Knowledge, to me, means the ability to learn the right things from experience, including the knowledge of objectives.

For instance, if I might digress for a moment, my elder daughter had many boy friends who, in the depths of the Depression, were coming out of college and looking for jobs just when jobs were the hardest things to obtain. Some of these young men paid me the dubious compliment of asking my help in getting a job. To those who answered my question, "What do you want to do?" with "I will do anything, I will even dig ditches," I said I was sorry but I could not help.

However, when a young man knew what line of business he was seeking, I was sometimes able to help him get started.

Enthusiasm—this, in short, is to get a real kick out of what you are doing, over and above the money you are getting out of it.

Common sense—I have found that common sense is the most uncommon, the rarest element in human beings. Common sense, to me, means the ability to make the right decision more often than not.

How did I begin? Well, when I came back from Santa Barbara, I joined Averell in a shipbuilding venture. Averell had been involved in shipbuilding during the war, and this was why he had not been called into the services, as shipbuilding was a vital defense industry. Some time before, Averell had taken a small, very small interest in a classmate's business of developing copra in the Philippines. Copra is what you get from coconuts. This young man had trouble, however, in finding ships in which he could transport the copra to markets. Averell said, "Why don't you buy a couple of ships yourself? If you do, I'll help you to find the money." This was when Europe was at war so there were no suitable ships to be found. Averell decided that, if ships were so scarce, and so important, shipbuilding must be a good business.

Averell was fortunate enough to be able to surround himself with people who knew how to build ships, and he started. He got all the encouragement he needed from

54

the government, and he started his first shipyard from scratch at Chester, Pennsylvania, not far from Philadelphia, to build merchant vessels.

This was where I first went when I returned from Santa Barbara, and it was great training in what made things click. I was intrigued. Eventually, I joined my brother in the financial end of the shipbuilding business, and we flourished into the middle of the 1920s.

Somewhere along the line, we bought control of an old, well-known shipyard, William Cramp and Sons, Ship and Engine Building Company, in Philadelphia. This also flourished for some years, until we got overbuilt and sea transport in general went into a period of decline. Later, we liquidated our holdings in the Chester plant, but kept Cramp's because it manufactured other things such as turbines and large electrical appliances.

Jumping ahead many years to World War II, when shipping once again was very important, we were asked by the government to construct naval vessels in the yards. Cramp's got a contract to build some cruisers; I was somewhat active in this phase and we did deliver six cruisers to the United States Navy. After the war, however, the business again declined, but the government said they wanted the yard as a standby in the event of an emergency. So we sold Cramp's and thus we divested ourselves of all shipbuilding activity.

Then Averell gave me desk room in an investment firm which he had started called W. A. Harriman & Co., Inc. There again I was able to learn a little bit about how business was run. This was at 120 Broadway, and later at 39 Broadway, New York City.

One day in the early 1920s, a man approached me and

told me that there was a young genius up in Ogdensburg, New York, who had a small company up there supplying fertilizers and pesticides and so on, and it all sounded very interesting. So, being young and brash, I invested in it, and I soon found I had a bear by the tail. It took a lot more than I had thought to keep the thing going, a lot more effort and a lot more money.

In the end, I reorganized this little company at Ogdensburg. Finding a business, running it, is difficult enough. Often the most difficult problem seems to be finding the right name for it. We had gone through hundreds of possibilities before somebody had the brilliant inspiration of "Bob White." And, as that would make everybody think of agricultural products, we called the thing the Bob White Chemical Company.

We had a rather rocky time with Bob White. Not much money was involved in it, really, but we kept it going, and then we looked for additional products, and somebody sold us the idea of a liquid that you could put into automobile tires to seal up punctures. Well, in those days, automobile tires were very vulnerable, and we added the anti-leak liquid to our product line.

But suddenly everything started to go downhill, and I think the word that caused me to liquidate the company came when an irate customer wrote in with the gory details of a blowout. It seems that he had the blowout just as he was driving past the village policeman. Our liquid not only did not work in a blowout but it spurted out and drenched the cop. The man had to buy the policeman a new uniform. Somehow that did it and I cleaned up the Bob White Chemical Company.

This was, however, an excellent experience for me. I

think it was worth all the money I lost in the enterprise. It taught me, firstly, not to believe everything anybody said, and secondly, it gave me the gamut of conventional business training in production, management and sales.

Then a man by the name of Tench, a partner in a firm of engineers named Terry and Tench, came to see me with a plan to build a vehicular bridge across the Hudson River. This was in the days when the only crossing of the Hudson south of Albany was by ferryboat. Even in the 1920s there were a great many automobiles, and a great many traffic jams. There were particularly long lines waiting for the ferryboats, and on Sundays and holidays, the lines would sometimes extend for fifty miles. The new idea was sound because there was a very obvious need for a vehicular bridge across the Hudson south of Albany.

Since I lived on the west side of the Hudson, the idea appealed to me immensely. Terry and Tench had already obtained a charter from the State of New York to build a bridge and operate it for thirty years, at the end of which period the bridge would become the property of the state. The site designated in the charter was at Bear Mountain, a little south of West Point. There was no difficulty in this case in finding a name for the product. It was to be the Bear Mountain Bridge. This span was to be 1,632 feet long, much greater than any suspension bridge previously built.

So the financing of the Bear Mountain Bridge, such a new kind of enterprise, was another matter. I thought that first mortgage bonds could probably be sold to the public, as a speculative investment, but the equity money

57

was something else again. The possible purchasers of this higher-risk item were limited to public-spirited citizens who understood the situation and were willing to make a big bet. So I thought that the first mortgage bonds would be $3 million and the income bonds, which were really the equity, would be $1.5 million. With them would go 60 per cent of the common stock as a package.

Well, this was the first time I really had a salesman's job, and I called on an awful lot of people. I even made a trip to Daytona Beach, Florida, where John D. Rockefeller was wintering. I never got to see him, but I did see Raymond Fosdick, his man of affairs, and he subscribed to the venture. In fact, I did succeed in getting the financing done, and then to my horror I found that the price of steel had increased beyond the amount of money we had raised.

So I became an engineer for the first time in my life. I had an idea. I reasoned that a suspension bridge, as Bear Mountain Bridge would be, hung from wires that crossed from the tops of towers, and the word "hung" is used advisedly. I found that if we reduced the height of our bridge towers by some twenty-five feet, and ran the wires under the road level, we could make it. The idea worked very well indeed. We were able to save enough steel to keep the bridge within our budget. Why other suspension bridge builders have continued to use the more expensive method is beyond me.

Then we had a race against time to get the bridge finished. It was getting into October. The question was, should we try to lay the concrete for the roadway then, or wait until spring to avoid the frost. But we decided to take a chance and expedite construction, and we did beat the heavy frost and open the bridge on time in November 1924.

I want to say one thing—I am never going to be a construction worker. One time during the work, after the wires had been strung, I thought I would walk out onto the partly built bridge. It was on a little narrow-plank footpath, less than three feet wide. I got out a couple of hundred yards and then I looked down. I thought, what the hell am I doing here? I did manage to keep my nerve and walked back without getting down on my hands and knees, but I must say I felt like it. I still do not understand how these construction workers can walk their narrow beams, thirty or forty or a hundred stories high, without having conniption fits.

The building of the Bear Mountain Bridge also entailed the construction of a three-mile road on the east bank of the Hudson, from the bridgehead to the main road. This was very precipitous country, overlooking the New York Central railroad tracks, and the road was really a construction accomplishment of its own. We could not blast away heavily and have everything fall onto the railroad tracks. But we got it done.

Then, believe it or not, an inadequate number of people used the bridge. It was a little out of the direct traffic patterns. We had to charge what were then high rates, a dollar a car, and always the question was whether we should reduce the toll. If we cut it in half, would we get more than twice as many customers?

However, we did make enough money to pay our interest to both classes of bondholders, but the stock never got any dividends. Finally, the state bought the bridge, rather than wait for the charter term to take effect.

So the outcome was that everybody, including the stockholders, got their money back with interest, and the Hudson was shown to be bridgeable. Once again, I learned an awful lot, and I think I did contribute to the good of the country, and I had a lot of fun, as usual.

The principal figure in the early phase of Averell's and my life continued to be our mother. She backed us morally and sometimes financially. She was really a remarkable lady. My father had left everything to her in one of the shortest wills that has ever been drawn. I think it was nineteen words long, or something like that. Exactly how it read I forget, but it was something like, "I leave everything I have to my wife, Mary Williamson Harriman, and appoint her my executor." That was about all it was. And that sufficed in those days.

Today, with much less to dispose of, my own will is something like twenty-five pages long, mostly gobbledygook, with a lot of technical, legalistic phrases that mean exactly what my father said in nineteen words.

At any rate, my mother did have the responsibility for settling my father's affairs and for handling his estate. How much was it? The amounts were hard to pin down but they were substantial. My mother was shattered for about a year after my father's death, but she settled down to make her own name in the world. She was a doer, just like my father.

For example, there were few organized charities in those days and charitable gifts were made for the most part on an ad hoc basis. When my father died, the newspapers were filled with stories of his supposedly inexhaustible wealth, and we received literally thousands of begging letters. Many of the letters were fakes, but many were unquestionably legitimate requests for help.

Then my mother turned her mailbag over to an organization equipped to examine and analyze these things, because the letters kept pouring in, and finally it was estimated that the requests exceeded the estate by three times, although most of them stressed that my mother would never miss the money.

Many years later, I came to the conclusion that it is difficult to make money; it is more difficult to keep it after you have made it; and the most difficult thing is to give money away intelligently and constructively. Anyway, my mother soon got going in several philanthropic programs, including the Association for the Improvement of the Condition of the Poor, and also an institute for the betterment of city government. Both of these organizations are still alive and going great guns.

She established in my father's memory the E. H. Harriman Award for safety on the railroads. Depending on the size of the railroads concerned, there were the gold, silver and bronze medals, and they are still coveted.

Fortunately, my mother had some very good advisers. Judge Lovett, who had succeeded my father as the head of the Union Pacific, was a stalwart supporter. A lawyer by the name of Charles Peabody had drafted my father's will and took care of his personal matters. He was also helpful to my mother as an anchor to windward.

Financial matters in those days were not really as complicated as they are now. For one thing, we did not have any analysts! The difference was brought home to me around 1940 when we were revamping the Tompkins Square Building of the Boys Club of New York, which entailed opening up the box embedded in the cornerstone laid in 1901. Among its contents was a newspaper of the day. The "financial page" consisted of one third of a column listing all the stocks traded that day! And the great majority were stocks of railroads!

But one event that did not help too much was that, in 1913, the Equitable Life Building at 120 Broadway burned down. With it went all the Union Pacific records and all the family records. But my mother opened a new office at 475 Fifth Avenue. She had a man of affairs, as they called him, and a couple of bookkeepers, and she used to go there quite frequently.

My mother was a great judge of people. She would listen to people she believed to be authentic. People who approached her with ideas that appealed to her, these she would support, and with very few exceptions these ventures were successful. She was interested in youth. She was interested in music. So she helped support a music-for-children idea, with children's concerts at Carnegie Hall on Saturday mornings. She did a good job in helping give kids a good taste for music, although she was never able to instill this in me.

She would have no patience for whatever went in those days for Women's Lib. She always thought the boys of the family should have their good times without being bothered by females. If we went to the family ranch in Idaho, for example, to camp or hunt, the boys would be given the right to camp and hunt, and the girls would stay at the ranch houses. The girls would ride and all the rest. We would commingle, so to speak. But if there was any question of the boys having a good time, they were going to have it in their own way without interference. She was very proud of my sisters, who were always making achievements of their own, and doing things on their own, but she thought this should not be at the expense of the male members of the family.

In her own life, she was gradually becoming an expert philanthropist, and we learned from her and resolved to carry on in her way.

There was no philanthropic enterprise in which she, and we, took greater pride than in our involvement in the Boys Club of New York. My father started the Boys Club in 1876 and there is a story about it that I do not think has ever been told, at least in print. It was before he married, and he had a young lady as a friend who was interested in a settlement house, the Wilson Mission School, on the Lower East Side. She cajoled my father into accompanying her down there one afternoon, and while she was busy about the building, he was having a chat with the matron, a Miss Huntington. Suddenly a brick crashed through the window and landed at my father's feet. This startled him, but the matron did not seem perturbed. She said, "Don't bother, Mr. Harriman. That's just one of the naughty boys out on the street. They have nothing better to do."

That single brick turned out to be the cornerstone of the Boys Club of New York, because my father said, "Let's see if we can't do something about it."

So my father induced a half a dozen of his male friends to come down to the district with him one or two nights a week. They rented the basement of a building, put in some games and reading matter, and taught the boys to box so as to lure them off the streets.

Well, the going was pretty slow until the cop on the beat told the boys it was all right and they had better go down and find out what was going on. In those days, the cop had a position in the community, instead of being called a pig, and the idea caught on.

At first, it was called the Tompkins Square Boys Club, and it was the first organization of its kind in the United States. It was strictly a place of recreation where the East Side boys could drop in and meet one another, talk, sing and play indoor games rather than roister on the streets.

Gradually over the years the number of boys who visited the club on a regular basis increased from forty or fifty to one hundred or more and then to a thousand or more, and the success of the Boys Club of New York was almost unbelievable.

My father's career as a railroad builder and administrator was concentrated, as I have pointed out, in a relatively brief period. But he was the predominant figure in the Boys Club for thirty-three years, more than half his lifetime. One year, when the Club fell more than $11,000 short of meeting its operating expenses, my father made good the deficit and notified the trustees that he would contribute each year one half of the total sum they raised from other sources, an arrangement my mother continued until about 1925.

I should have mentioned that, early in 1901, the organization had moved into a new home. My father had purchased land on the corner of Avenue A and Tenth Street and laid the cornerstone of a five-story building with all the accouterments to delight a kid's heart. He retained a mortgage of $113,000 on this building.

1. "The Admiral" (Roland Harriman) in Alaska, 1899.

2. The author's father, E. H. Harriman, at his desk in Union Pacific offices about 1907.

3. "Old" Arden Homestead about 1905.

4. The author's mother in her later years.

So the whole thing was growing like Topsy, and it was exciting for me to go down there with my father to see what was going on. They had an Englishman named Francis Tabor who had the great idea, as superintendent, that dramatics were especially good for young people. Tabor was particularly interested in Gilbert and Sullivan, and in 1902 forty boys from seven to fourteen years of age gave a very creditable performance of *Pinafore*. This was followed in later years by other Gilbert and Sullivans. The Boys Club performances were so good they moved uptown, as the saying goes, once a year to give a benefit performance.

So, as I say, I started about the turn of the century to be aware of this Boys Club, and I noticed that my father got the gangs off the streets as gangs. They would come into the clubhouse and form clubs within the Club, so to speak, maintaining that gang spirit young people seem to enjoy. And each of these inner clubs would get a volunteer leader who would meet with them twice a week and counsel them in life's wisdom, or what have you. The rest of the time the boys would spend in the gymnasium or doing whatever they chose.

Another very successful aspect of the Boys Club in these early years was its camp on Long Island, located on twenty-five acres of unimproved land near Jamesport.

The year after my father's death, my mother canceled the $113,000 mortgage my father had held on the building at Avenue A and Tenth Street, and presented it to the Boys Club as my father's last gift.

In 1921, I became formally involved in the Boys Club when I was elected a trustee. One of the reasons for the Club's continued success was that we have always had

65

an exceptional Board of Trustees. I want to emphasize this because, to my mind, the Boys Club trustees have the best idea of how to be a trustee. We established the principle that a trustee should either work, give, get or get out. That was very definitely the policy that was adhered to then and now.

Then, too, we have a splendid group of women who serve on our so-called "Ladies' Board." Started in the 1920s by Gladys, this group has steadily increased their influence so that now they are a most important part of our whole set-up.

Charles Sabin, who had become president of the Club, was perhaps the finest money-raiser in the country. It is not too much to say that he would attend a social dinner and weep on the shoulders of the ladies on either side of him as he told them about the boys on the Lower East Side. Sure enough, usually the next day, big checks would arrive from the importuned ladies.

The Boys Club staff could also produce results. We soon had as many as seventy-five or eighty young volunteer leaders, working night after night, and kids were coming off the streets from all over. By golly, we were even informed by the New York City Police Department that our district now had the lowest rate of juvenile delinquency in the city.

In due course, a new and commodious building was opened on East 111th Street, known as the Jefferson Park Branch, on the fringe of Harlem. There was a colossal need there and we enjoyed another formidable success. If you can believe it, our total enrollment reached eight thousand boys.

Well, then came the great crash of 1929, and shortly thereafter Charles Sabin died. They asked me to become president and I was very happy to accept. But I soon discovered that many of our generous contributors had died physically or financially and the Boys Club was getting into serious difficulties on the financial side. I laid the facts before the trustees.

As I recall, on a budget of $150,000 a year—and that was up from $10,000 a year at the turn of the century—we had a mortgage on all the properties of $100,000 and loans at the bank of $60,000, with an annual rate of operating loss of $25,000 or $30,000 a year. This could not go on because we had a very small endowment fund, and so I told the trustees that if we were to continue to exist, we had to go out as a team and raise the money. I had three resignations. The rest of us, more than forty of us, really went to work around town. We cleaned up the mortgage, balanced the budget and suffered no interruption of our work with the boys. Today, the Boys Club of New York budget is approximately $1.5 million, colossally larger than it was in my father's day.

One of the principal benefactors was Victor Morowitz, a lawyer, who had been associated with my family and was very much interested in the Boys Club. When he died, he left the Club the sum of $4 million. The income from half of this bequest was to be used for ordinary purposes, and that from the other half for a program of higher education for promising youngsters. This last has also been an outstandingly successful facet of the Boys Club of New York. Something like one hundred and fifty Boys Club boys are now attending preparatory schools or universities, and others have gone on to graduate schools, with help from this brilliant bequest.

I have many wonderful memories of my years with the Boys Club, and if the chronology might seem to be a little blurred, I trust the feeling will not be. For example, there was a story about the Prince of Wales, who later became the Duke of Windsor.

The Prince of Wales, on one of his visits to the United States in the 1920s, asked to see the Boys Club. So I took him down to Tompkins Square and showed him around. Maybe it was in the 1930s, but it was before he became king. He was a fascinating fellow, very attractive. He had a memory for names and faces far superior to that of any headwaiter I ever met. When we entered the Club, we went into the library, and the librarian had put a recent book about the Prince on display. The Prince said, "Look at page 230," or whatever page it was. And right on that page was a picture of the Prince, a shot of him visiting General Douglas MacArthur, the superintendent at West Point.

Well, it was at least ten years before I met the Prince of Wales again, now the Duke of Windsor, and that was in a dark room at the Links Club. He was walking by, and he saw me. Without hesitation he said, "Hello, Harriman, how are you?" And he added, "How is the Boys Club?"

Just a few days after that, he called me up and said, "This is my birthday, and my friends have sent me a most enormous birthday cake, a four-tiered thing. Unfortunately, the Duchess and I are going home this afternoon and won't be able to enjoy it. Do you suppose the boys at the Boys Club would like it?" I said, "They surely would." So I sent for it, and we sent the word out along the highways and byways for the boys to come to the Club and have a piece of the Duke of Windsor's cake.

Fortunately, just before the young throng arrived, one of the staff people at the Club happened to poke the lowest tier of the cake. To his consternation he found it was made of cardboard. In fact, the whole cake was cardboard, apart from a little bitty cake on top. What to do? The staff sent out to all the bakeries within the radius, and bought up all the cakes and goodies in sight. The boys were not disappointed that the Duke's cake was a disappointment.

Then there was that story about Mr. X—there is always a Mr. X—and his wife, who were attending a speakeasy. They stayed until the wee hours when a young kid came in to sell the early edition of the morning newspapers. Mr. X and his wife bought a newspaper and engaged the young man in conversation. When Mr. X asked where he lived, and found out he lived in the vicinity of one of the Boys Clubs, Mr. X said, "Oh, you're a member of the Boys Club?" The young man said, "No, my ma won't let me. She says the kids are too tough."

Mrs. X then remarked, "Well, you tell your mother that you met a lady who said the Boys Club is just the place for you. You'll have the time of your life and you'll find the other kids are no tougher than you are."

The young man said, "Fine, then, and shall I tell my ma I met the lady in a bar?"

Louis Lefkowitz, the attorney general of the State of

New York, is a Boys Club alumnus, and very proud of it. So was Irving Berlin and the Kriendlers of the "21" Club. So is a barber downtown who has interested his customers in the Boys Club, interested enough to contribute more than $50,000 over the past several years. So was a young man named Peter Capra, who was born in Italy, came over here as a kid with his family, became a member of the Tompkins Square Branch and resolved to excel. On his own account, he earned a scholarship to Andover, and then to Yale.

Peter Capra then returned to the Boys Club and became a junior staff member. He was outstanding. Next he went into business and became, within five or six years, a vice-president of one of the largest department stores in the city. He married and had children. When his father-in-law went bankrupt in the great crash, Peter Capra left his job and put his father-in-law's business back on its feet. At that point, he came back to us and said, "I have proved myself, and now I want to come back to the Boys Club." He had indeed, and he did indeed— as director. Until his untimely death, he was as outstanding a director as he had been a staff member, and as a boy.

All in all, well over half a million kids have been members of the Club and felt its influence.

Where we are today is symbolized, perhaps, by an artist's compilation in my office of Boys Club members in 1946. In his group of ten boys, there were Nordics, Irish, Italians, Jewish boys, only one black. If an artist drew the same picture today, there might be one white boy, and the other nine would be black or of Hispanic origin.

The total number of members is approximately the same as it was twenty or thirty years ago, perhaps a little less, but we are doing a great deal more for them. We still have the Tompkins Square and the Jefferson Park branches, and another one near Grand Street, in downtown Manhattan. We have a camp of about four thousand acres in the lower Catskill Mountains. We are also providing greater service for the boys in organized guidance and counseling. To put it bluntly, families are not organized the way they used to be, and frequently there are no fathers around.

We have also branched out into a certain amount of what might be called health follow-up. We have established a dental clinic, staffed by professionals, who are volunteers. We give the boys a health and dental examination when they become members, and the boys who need help can get it for a nominal fee. This fee is far below cost, but it is important because the boys realize they are paying for help, and not getting something for nothing.

There is also a token membership dues of twenty-five cents a month with an additional charge for attendance at camp. This is a pittance in the budget, but its importance is something else. The boys pay dues just as we do to social or athletic clubs. They know that some angel makes up the difference, but they feel that the clubhouse is their own.

President Sabin once said that the creed of the Boys Club was "Clean living and fair dealing." That is not bad. In fact, it is very good. We do run a kind of three-ring circus, all with the idea of giving the boys a good time off the streets, while helping teach them how to become good citizens. There are groups involved in music, dramatics, basketball, running, wrestling, boxing, drawing, painting and other pursuits. We teach them fair play in competition, and they are good losers as well as modest winners.

Fundamentally, and I believe this sincerely, kids nowadays are basically unchanged. To quote Peter Capra, "No boy is born bad." They are doing strange things that might seem to be deplorable. But kids are still kids, and they are influenced by the people surrounding them. They can be influenced for good and for bad, and that is why the Boys Club is so important. We provide an influence that will help move young people in the right direction. This is a long, long process that will go on perhaps for all time.

So, there it is, and the Boys Club, along with other experiences in my life, has been great fun. We have good people, fine people, working together, with no jealousies, no friction, no squabbles. I think that is the reason the trustees and the staff and everybody else work harmoniously and get a kick out of it.

The thing I am most proud of is that my father started the whole thing nearly one hundred years ago, just because some kid threw a brick through a window, and it landed at his feet.

CHAPTER IV: MY FAVORITE PEOPLE

New York, January 2nd, 1931

Gentlemen:

We take pleasure in advising you that effective January 1, 1931, the businesses of Messrs. Brown Brothers & Co., Harriman Brothers & Co., and W. A. Harriman & Co., Inc., have been united in the copartnership firm of Brown Brothers Harriman & Co.

Our merger with the Brown Brothers firm was, of course, a very important step in my life, and there was a story from an old western railroad survey that seemed as appropriate to me then as it does now. The story—I suppose it was a wisecrack really—went like this: "If the Brown brothers went camping because they wanted to know if a railroad should be built, E. H. Harriman built a railroad because he went camping." And if there was a great deal of speculation that the Brown Brothers, with their venerable, dynamic tradition, and the Harriman interests, with what was termed our size and vitality, constituted an ideal partnership, then I am sure the speculation was justified.

To put it more succinctly, they had enjoyed a long and honorable career. We had a short and honorable career. Now we were to be partners.

The first thing I want to emphasize about my own part in this merger is that there was an intimate friendship between the younger partners of Brown Brothers and Averell and myself, and also, of course, with Knight Woolley, the managing partner of our firm Harriman Brothers, and Prescott Bush, vice-president of W. A. Harriman & Co. Many of us had attended the same preparatory schools, and practically all of us had been at Yale together.

Some of the Brown Brothers partners were nearing retirement age and, naturally, when they would retire, they would withdraw their partnership holdings over a period of time. Therefore, it had become desirable for the younger partners to replenish the capital that would be withdrawn. On the other hand, my brother and I were young in the field of finance and Brown Brothers had its long, honorable record, with a great deal of current financial acumen. It had been founded in 1818 by the original Brown, first as linen merchants and then, to finance the linen operations, as a banking establishment. There is, today, the seventh generation of Browns in the firm.

Through just a series of mutual explorations, in which we discussed the prospects of getting together under the same roof, the merger appeared to become a most desirable thing, jointly, and so we decided to do it. I want to emphasize that the merger discussion all started long before the country began to move into the Depression. So the four or five older Brown Brothers partners retired and the rest of us joined forces. My brother and I and our firm introduced some new capital into the merged firm and we started business together.

In other words, this was a happy marriage arrangement, not a shotgun wedding by any manner or means. In fact, things went so well it seemed that our one difficulty was a confusion of names. There was also, at that time, a Harriman and Company, brokers, which had originally been started by my father and an uncle, from which my father had withdrawn as he became increasingly involved in railroad affairs. Then there was a Harriman National Bank, which was run by a nephew of my father's, and this was one of the casualties of the Depression. In fact, its failure was about to be announced at almost the same time as the formation of our new Brown Brothers Harriman & Co. Fortunately, we were able to arrange that the news media made it clear there was no connection between us.

Later on, we had some more difficulty with names. When the laws were passed in 1934 prohibiting banks from engaging in the investment banking business, the issuing business, we had to make a major adjustment. The original Brown Brothers had been engaged primarily in the banking business, but was of some importance in the issuing business. Our W. A. Harriman & Co., Inc., had been in the issuing business.

So, in 1934, when we were told to divorce the two sides of our merged business, four of our partners joined the officers of the National City Company, which was owned by the National City Bank, in the formation of a joint issuing business. We felt it was important to identify this new outfit in terms of reputation for quality, and it was called Brown Harriman & Co., Inc. Now we had Brown Brothers Harriman & Co., the bankers, and Brown Harriman & Co., Inc., in the issuing business. This was all extremely confusing and nobody could distinguish who was who. After two or three years of agony, we solved the problem by inducing the latter to change its name to Harriman Ripley & Co. Ripley was one of the City Bank people, and the use of his name helped alleviate some of the trouble.

For years to come, however, there was still some confusion in spite of all our efforts. Fortunately, Harriman Ripley & Co. was merged first with Drexel & Co. and then with an additional group, after which the name Harriman was completely dropped.

At this point, I should make it clear that Brown Brothers Harriman & Co. was involved in matters of greater moment than the selection of the names of the businesses. It is not my purpose in these reminiscences, however, to engage in a sort of exposé, a now-it-can-be-told extravaganza of the so-called secrets of a private banking institution. Nor would I, in any case, as the essence of a business such as ours is confidentiality and trust between partners. Another point is that these reminiscences are addressed, in a sense, to many of the splendid men and women who were involved in these affairs and know what was going on anyway.

I seek to contribute here, as elsewhere in this book, some personal thoughts.

There are many stories surrounding this famous Brown Brothers Harriman merger in 1931, but there was no single moment when nothing became everything, so to speak. I have said, for example, that I had been a friend of Robert Lovett's, who had been admitted to partnership in Brown Brothers & Co. in 1926.

Then there was Ellery S. James, the son of a New York lawyer, who joined Brown Brothers & Co. in 1919. Ellery and I had been friends since before prep school and he was one of the friends we took along on that cruise of the yacht *Sultana* through the Panama Canal. He had been a classmate of mine at Yale. Ellery and I talked in the mid-1920s about bringing Brown Brothers, into which he had been admitted to partnership in 1925, and our Harriman interests under a single roof.

It was probably in a continuation of this original chat with me that Ellery brought up the matter with Prescott Bush and Knight Woolley. It is true that this celebrated conversation took place in a drawing room of a parlor car on the New Haven Railroad en route to a Yale reunion. Other partners of Brown Brothers of our vintage at Yale were Lawrence G. Tighe and, in particular, Charles D. Dickey.

Later in 1930, things came to a head when Ellery took up the matter formally with Knight, and with Thatcher M. Brown, a member of the Brown family and a partner. Everything was all wrapped up by the turn of the year.

So the real story about this merger was a joining of forces by people who thought alike and liked each other, and it was a congenial setup.

For example, we had a wonderful relationship with Thatcher Brown, despite the difference in our ages. We all thought Thatcher was a doll. And that was always one great thing about the firm of Brown Brothers Harriman. We never had a senior partner, so designated. It was true that, because of his age and reputation, we deferred to Thatcher in many respects. To the outside, he might have been considered the senior partner, but inside, no.

Over the years, we have had no senior or junior partners. We have nobody who takes precedence over anybody else, except by mutual admiration and respect. If we ever had an internal arrangement with a title, which we do not, the closest might be a designated "Managing Partner." This is the partner through whom, by habit, we channel the day-to-day business of the firm. Two incumbents of this amorphous position in recent years have been, in turn, Thomas McCance and John Madden, both of whom started their banking careers with our firm.

Maybe the closest to a sharp word I ever heard spoken —we of course have our differences of opinion and we argue in a friendly manner—was in the early 1950s. Knight Woolley had been working awfully hard and he began taking some Mondays off. After two or three weeks of this, Prescott Bush met him in the hallway and said, "Knight, why aren't you here on Mondays? Do you think you're senior partner?"

Brown Brothers Harriman is the only large commercial bank in the United States which is owned and operated by a partnership instead of by a corporation, has a seat on the New York Stock Exchange and is authorized to carry on its banking business across state lines. And it is bound in the concept of a partnership of unlimited liability of all the partners. We are really all in it together.

In fact, we are all in it together, sink or swim. And that has been a good talking point when we approach prospective customers. We are not simply custodians. We are not managing stockholders' money. We are managing our own money, and that is quite a difference.

I do not think it is really any secret but Averell and I were originally the major capital contributors. However, the other partners, plus the new, younger partners, have also made money over the years from our operations, and they have plowed a substantial part of this back into the firm. What is the result? Today, the other partners together own twice as much of the capital of the firm as Averell and I do. Of this we are very proud.

This demonstrates the stability of the partners and their own confidence in the future of the firm. They are working for themselves as they work for our customers. They are reaping the benefits of their own efforts and of the association of all the partners. This contributes in large measure to the success of the enterprise.

Another unusual element of the partnership is that, with few exceptions, important exceptions, all the partners have grown up in the business. This is a great strength in our organization because every employee of the bank, to use a Napoleonic phrase, feels that he has a marshal's baton in his knapsack.

It was at the end of the eighteenth century that Alexander Brown, a successful linen merchant in Belfast, decided to relocate across the Atlantic in Baltimore. He imported linen for the most part, and exported cotton, tobacco and other commodities, building up what would nowadays be termed an excellent credit reputation on both sides of the Atlantic. He developed a bill-of-exchange business that was successful enough to supersede the linen business.

Alexander Brown's four sons were the original Brown Brothers. One, John A. Brown, started the Brown Brothers firm in Philadelphia in 1818. Eight years later, the firm opened an office in New York City, and in 1833 it moved to the corner of Wall Street and Hanover Street. It is still there. The Boston offices were established in 1844.

Meanwhile, William Brown, the eldest of the brothers, had returned to England in 1819. There he established a very prosperous branch in Liverpool, which would subsequently become Brown Shipley & Co. Until World War I, the relationship of the two partnerships was extremely close, with partners of one firm also partners of the other. Even after the taxation problems of international partnerships forced a legal separation during World War I, the firms continued to work very closely and effectively with one another.

Brown Brothers performed an inestimable service in the development of national and international commerce. The acceptance and handling of commercial bills of exchange was as fundamental then as now. The firm dominated the scene to the extent that its posted rates of foreign exchange, known as "Brown's Posted Rates"—they were actually posted outside the building at 59 Wall Street —were *the* rates of exchange.

Similarly, Brown Brothers originated the traveler's letter of credit. Among the old relics preserved in our offices is the original letter of credit issued to President Woodrow Wilson for his historic mission to the peace conference at Versailles in 1919 and the one issued to Charles Lindbergh for his historic flight to Paris.

From its position at the very heart of national and international commerce, Brown Brothers was involved in many colorful episodes. It was at George Brown's house in Baltimore that a leading group of citizens met to organize the Baltimore and Ohio Railroad, our nation's first railroad company, and he served as the treasurer. The firm and most of the partners had interest in the late 1850s in the American-flag Collins Line of steamships, which won the blue riband of the Atlantic away from the Cunard Steamship Company before it suffered a tragic series of shipwrecks.

The Brown Brothers firm survived the Civil War, and this was quite a feat because much of its business had concerned the export of cotton from the southern states. Brown Brothers also emerged from the financial panics of 1873, 1893 and 1907 in characteristically stable style.

As I have said, our original W. A. Harriman & Co., Inc., had been organized little more than ten years before the merger. Under Averell's first-rate leadership, fortified by that of G. H. Walker, president from 1920 to 1930, and by that of Pres Bush, the firm had grown rapidly and strongly. We were one of the first United States investment organizations to help rebuild European industry after World War I.

Harriman Brothers & Co., set up in 1927, reflected the particular determination and expertise of Knight Woolley, its managing partner. Knight started his business career with the American Exchange National Bank whence we were lucky enough to get him for our new firm. He started with four employees in a single room. In less than four years, it had moved twice into larger premises, and had seventy employees. Knight was such an authority on banker's acceptances that he wrote the *A.B.C. of Banker's Acceptances,* published by the American Acceptance Council in 1924. Incidentally, banker's acceptances are one of the highest forms of commercial credit, in which banks substitute their own widely known credit for that of their customer. This credit, instead of cash, secures the movement of trade.

By the time of the merger, Harriman Brothers was doing very well in acceptances and foreign exchange, and had a seat on the New York Stock Exchange. We had only expected to be a small bank, but by that time we knew a lot of people and industries, and so on, and they were friendly to us, and we thought we could be of service to them and they to us. And so this brief historical account comes full circle.

Outside of the fact that our new partnership worked splendidly, we had no formal routine. In those first days, we had a small group of partners, nine in number, most of whom sat in the Partners' Room. This is an old-fashioned countinghouse type of establishment, with rolltop desks, and the location of the partnership has been in the same spot for generations. The building structure on the site has been changed, but the spot has not. So we partners were able to yell across at one another, so to speak, if there was any problem we wanted advice about from one of our congenial colleagues.

Then we had weekly partners' meetings, fixed meetings, at which results were discussed and future plans made. This was also a free, give-and-take exercise in communications. Each of the partners had his own niche and was supposed to make sense of what he was doing and report to all the others. For instance, we had pure and simple commercial banking, which Knight Woolley was mostly responsible for. Then we had the security end, in which we did, and still do, give investment advice to customers. Pres Bush was more or less in charge of the security end. We were and still are members of the Stock Exchange. We have never had a floor broker. We never had what they call a board room. We have no margin accounts. We buy and sell for the account of our customers.

I was more or less a roving partner, and this was a very easy, give-and-take affair. We had no organization chart as such. We understood what it was. Nothing was drawn out. I have always taken the position that an organization chart is nothing more or less than a guide of how you intend to function. I have talked about the dangers of square boxes—when they try to fit round people into those boxes, and it does not work, because personality is such an important part of any operation.

Sometimes I think that the great trouble in large organizations—and fortunately I have had much experience with large organizations—is the handling of communications between different partners or different executives. This is almost always a great block within a major organization, this communication between people who occupy positions of importance. I guess one trouble with the whole darned world, as we all recognize, is that scraps start because there has been not enough communication of a reasonable nature between the different chiefs of state. And, in our business, this ability to communicate is one of the principal advantages of remaining relatively small.

In our discussion with customers and potential customers we always point out the advantages of a compact organization where the partners are able to communicate and, to a great extent, can substitute one for another. Also, our potential customers know that our partners are risking their own money and, in truth, will sink or swim together. We have no outside directors or other associates so we can keep our relationships with customers on a strictly confidential basis.

Another advantage we offer is that we have the same partners on hand day after day, and customers can come in and talk. There is in fact a personal relationship. We do not have an ever shifting group of bank officers who are here today and gone tomorrow.

We have the usual managerial hierarchy below the partnership level, managers, deputy managers, security officers, bank officers and so on, but here again we stress continuity and long-term relationships of trust between our managers and our customers. I will concede that as part of the price of our growing there is less direct communication now between the partners and the staff than there used to be. On the other hand, I will add that our awareness of this trend has established in our minds a reluctance to grow beyond any size that we do not feel we can adequately handle. Deliberately, we have restricted ourselves to a small clientele of top-flight businesses and individuals.

We have a banking branch in Philadelphia, and another in Boston, with a partner in charge of each. Although there is now a prohibition against banks having branches in other states, we are able to do it since we were in operation in these cities before the ban was enacted. We have a security outlet in Chicago with a resident partner in an established office, but we cannot have a banking operation there because we opened up in Chicago after the ban was enacted. But one way or another, all our offices manage to maintain the atmosphere of a family group.

Consequently, we take the utmost care in staff recruitment. We go out and interview outstanding graduates of business administration colleges. On rare occasions we also talk with young people who walk in off the street, cold. We tell them we take on only six to ten young men each year, and we really do select them by our own feelings about their looks, their experience and the way they talk about their ambitions in life. It is a personal process. If accepted, they receive several months' training in various departments, and, as I have said, they have the chance of working up to become a partner in the firm, as several of them have done.

One of the interesting facets of Brown Brothers Harriman & Co. is that our foreign friends, our banking colleagues around the world, often send their young men over to us for a training course in our offices. We have had some remarkable examples of the effectiveness of this approach. Our young overseas friends get a good education and, in many cases, move on to become the heads of their banks overseas. Our own company benefits, of course, from these connections. Small wonder nowadays that we pay a lot of attention to these young fellows who come over and work with us for a while. Right now, we have them from England, France, Germany, Switzerland, Belgium, Holland and Sweden.

So we have a personal relationship with our overseas friends, as well as a business one. One reason we get on so well in this regard is that we deal with banks, and do not deal with national companies. In other words, we are not competitive with local banking institutions overseas. This has been a great strength and it still is. For example, we maintain an office in Switzerland from which we conduct no business other than to act as a liaison with our European banking friends and to accept and report execution of orders. It has worked out well.

Partners in Banking, in which the historian John A. Kouwenhoven tells the story of the first 150 years of the partnership, details a trip made by Thatcher Brown to Europe. The date of sailing was November 12, 1918, one day after the end of World War I. "It had been apparent for some weeks previous that the war was drawing to a close," Thatcher wrote, "and it became necessary to send a partner to Europe promptly to trade and negotiate out and settle many war casualties involving the shipment of commodities to Europe, and particularly to the Scandinavian countries under our Commercial Letters of Credit. . . . Of the numerous cases . . . only one resulted in a lawsuit and . . . we felt our trip was well worthwhile."

No doubt one reason for this result was the fact that Thatcher was welcomed at Stockholm by Marcus Wallenberg, executive director of the Enskilda Bank of Stockholm, at whose country estate Thatcher had been a guest five years previously. His Swedish friend took Thatcher to see King Gustav, who had wanted to meet, as he put it, "the first American businessman to reach Sweden since the end of the war."

Since then, there have been Wallenbergs among the young men working with us, and, as a matter of fact, one of our partners is the godfather of a member of the latest generation of Wallenbergs.

Today, when people comment that people-to-people exchanges are one of our best bets for international understanding and world peace, I know they are right. I know because we have been doing this for decades, and our partners continue to make frequent trips abroad to maintain our personal contacts.

Until 1932, Brown Brothers never issued a public statement of the condition of finances but since the merger we have felt it very desirable to do so. We would do this willingly, and now we are required as members of the New York State banking structure under the supervision of the State Banking Commission to issue such statements. These statements confirm that we are a fairly small frog in the big puddle.

When I am asked whether I have a preferred investment approach, I have to reply that I cannot generalize. Things change so quickly nowadays, and, of course, everything depends upon the requirements of the customer. If they want income, we give them one type of advice. This is obvious, but it is not obvious that there is no such thing as safety in the absolute sense.

The way I look at it, at the present time, is that the business of investment has become an extremely complicated affair. It is no longer possible for one man, even a small group of men, to keep track of what is going on, and this is why the so-called analysts have become so necessary and important. These men devote their time to one type of industry which they follow carefully, and then they follow a limited number of companies within that industry. We are somewhat at the mercy of the quality of the analysts because no partner can follow the myriad of investment opportunities without guidance from the analysts. As a firm, we do not try even to follow every listed security. We follow what we think we can do a good job on.

One thing we do try to read is market movement. And this is a most difficult task because market movement is always a result of how other people think and act. One never really knows what the other fellow is going to do. We have also learned that investors often have some weird reasons for their actions. It is very complicated, the market. We gauge the trend of finance nationally and internationally, and we try to judge what effect legislation will have on industry of one kind or another. But we never know what is going to come out of Washington. That again is a guessing game.

So it is like everything else, a matter of common sense —the ability to make the right decision more often than not.

The one thing we will not do is give casual advice. I have a shining example. In the spring of 1929, just a few months before the debacle, I ran into a funny fellow with whom my wife used to deal. He was a Canadian trapper, of all things, and he was at the house to pick up some furs she wanted cleaned, or stored, or something.

The Canadian trapper asked me, "Mr. Harriman, what do you think of the market?" I do not remember what I said, but the next year, after the crash, I ran into him again. He said this time, "Oh, Mr. Harriman, I can't thank you enough." I said, "What for?" He went on, "Don't you remember, a year ago I asked what you thought of the market, and you said, 'Not much.' So I sold everything I had."

Now, I might just as well have said offhandedly, "I think the market is great." So I learned at that moment never to give casual advice. Needless to say, when customers leave their account with us, and pay us to give them advice, so we can tell them when to sell and when to buy, then that is a different matter. This is not casual advice—and our recommendations are crafted as professionally as we are able. We think we do a good job in this situation. But we are not tipsters.

At Brown Brothers Harriman, our partners have served from time immemorial on directorships of national corporations where there is a quid pro quo. We believe this helps our partners gain knowledge of general business conditions and at the same time be of assistance to the companies on whose boards they sit.

In such a capacity I have served, in addition to the Union Pacific System, on boards of the Mutual Life Insurance Company of New York, the Anaconda Company, the American Bank Note Company and the Atlantic Mutual Insurance Company. The last two companies were old Brown Brothers accounts of many years' standing.

I do remember well the associations with which I have been identified over the years, and have found the time and attention I have given to these activities extremely valuable. I have met very fine people, I have learned a great deal about some very fine businesses and I have been, I hope, able to contribute to them in one way or another. This is all part and parcel of the well-rounded business experience that we encourage our partners to develop as much as they can.

During these years I was also able to undertake several

outside missions. Among these I was trustee of the American Museum of Natural History and the National Safety Council.

It was in 1934, as I remember, that I started work with the American Museum of Natural History. The treasurer had to resign because of the pressure of outside work, and he asked me to be the treasurer and to take his place as chairman of the Finance Committee. As such my work would have to do with the investment of the endowment fund. He told me, "You won't have any trouble. You'll just get some advice from some of our financial friends and you'll just put a rubber stamp on them."

This did not happen, because it was the Depression and nothing was easy—not even the museum business. For six years it was agonizing for us to make up our minds on what was the best thing to do. At one time one of our committee members threw up his hands and said, "I think the time has come when we should sell everything and invest in government bonds." Another member piped up and said, "Bill, are we responsible for having a good museum or a good endowment fund?"

For me, it was rewarding work, because we were able to muddle through and we still had a good-looking endowment fund while maintaining a museum that is still one of the very finest in the world.

Through these working years with Brown Brothers Harriman—and, as I shall say, with the Union Pacific Railroad and the American Red Cross—I refined my own working habits. I worked, at first, six days a week, then five days when the work was reduced and lately I'm down to three. There is a saying that you get more work out of a busy man than out of a part-time busy man.

It is all a question of how you organize your time and your capabilities, and how much time you spend on worrying about things, rightly or wrongly.

I found that I preferred to work rapidly, even at the risk of making mistakes, than to take my time and then make mistakes.

It was a bit like the advice an expert bridge player once gave his inept partner. He said, "Bill, play your cards quickly even though you pull the wrong card. Don't think and think and think and play the wrong card."

Again, there is the question of not undertaking more than you can actually handle. It ought to be possible to devote the time you have available to handling the matters that need attention. These ought to be handled in business hours.

I do not believe, except in exceptional cases, that you should take your business home with you. Often, this is "so-called" business and it is not as important as you think it is. You have to think about business during leisure hours, certainly, but I have no sympathy for the people who go home laden with a briefcase full of work that they should have completed in their business hours. With organization, it can be done.

I also think you should be able to have the will power to turn your mind away from a problem when you find your concentration is slipping. When I was in school, I got some good advice in this regard from the family doctor. He told me, "If you are studying something and you begin to get fuzzy, quit it, and do something else. Then, when your mind is clearer, go back to the original problem." And I have found in business as well as at school that it is refreshing simply to think about something else.

I do not think business executives ought to bone up like the old-style schoolboys, with towels wrapped around their heads. That is for the birds. And I noticed that, even though I had to turn over many matters to my partners, I did not slip up on any responsibilities that were placed in my hands.

Now, that is a broad statement and, of course, I made many mistakes, many more than I should have, but I did not make them because of the pressure of work or an unwise allotment of time. The word is "delegation," and I believe in it, although it all depends on how good the people are to whom you delegate responsibility. As I always say, I have superb partners and associates.

So we are aware at Brown Brothers Harriman that there are rapid changes in all kinds of industries and we have to be as alert as we can be to these changes. Bob Lovett wrote a wonderful article about thirty-five years ago, and the title was never truer. His title was "Gilt-Edged Insecurity." Bob proved that what is a blue chip today might be a loss leader tomorrow. That is one of the fascinations of life.

Fortunately, there are still a lot of young fellows who want to go into a bank, and those who want to go into industry, and others who want to take up a profession.

In talking about the railroad business, it often seemed during the 1920s that there was little, if any, attraction for a young man to go into it. I remember distinctly that I had a talk with old Judge Lovett, Bob's father, who was still the head of Union Pacific. He advised me definitely not to go into the railroad business because there was no future in it. He said it was regulated from Washington, and there was no longer the scope for imagination and ability that there had been in my father's day.

That situation was too bad, because in a few years the railroad business really needed top-notch leaders and they were lacking. Other types of industry go through similar phases. One day they are popular, hot, and tomorrow they are not. Perhaps they will come back, and perhaps they will not.

What I would say now to an aspirant who wanted to go into the banking business is that in the banking business you do—and this is very important—deal with a broad spectrum of life. You deal with people and their hopes and problems and that can be fascinating. You deal with companies, and these are people, too. And you are making a contribution very definitely to the growth and well-being of the economy and the country as a whole. You make it possible for people to carry on.

For example, a few years back, we had a customer, a small customer, at Brown Brothers Harriman. I believe he was in the wool brokerage business. And he would borrow a few thousand dollars from time to time, pay it back, borrow it again and so on. He was a good type of small customer. Well, one day, he came in again and told the manager who was handling his account, "I want to borrow $15,000." The manager replied, "Oh, for that amount, I'll have to take it up with the Credit Committee and they'll want a statement from you."

Our customer scratched his head for a minute. Then he replied, "Tell them I'm very optimistic."

In 1934 when we concentrated on being a bank we had nine partners and a staff of about two hundred. Now there are, by golly, twenty-nine partners and about one thousand staff. I have outlived a lot of the original top staff and, of course, quite a few have retired. Unfortunately, two of our original partners, Ellery James and Prescott Bush, have been lost to us—and what a loss they were.

Well, anyway, whenever I think about all these people, past and present, with whom I have so closely worked over so many years, I continue to thank God for my good fortune in being able to do business with those whom I admire and respect so tremendously.

This is why I continue to use the word "enthusiasm" in my definition of what is really needed in a job. You can only be enthusiastic if you are happy with what you are doing and with whom you *are* doing it.

The word is "fun." I look back over all the trials and tribulations and successes in the firm of Brown Brothers Harriman and I conclude that it has been fun from start to finish.

CHAPTER V: CRISIS—CRISIS— CRISIS

As we moved through the 1930s, the Depression bit more deeply into the national economy, much more deeply. The stock market had broken overnight, but general business had not declined automatically. The creeping paralysis of our national morale did not reach its crisis until several years afterward. In fact, the thing that really gave us a jolt at Brown Brothers Harriman was the *Stillhalte* economic problem in Austria. We were international bankers and the *Stillhalte* temporarily embarrassed us and caused us to show red figures for a number of years. However, we survived it, and we learned as partners how to weather a storm together.

In the first months of the New Deal, the Depression was so severe that some 12 million people were out of work, farm foreclosures were at a high and heavy industries were operating at little more than one third of capacity. It was a ghastly time all around. Nobody knew just what was going to happen, or when, and it was distressing as well as disturbing to see the misery that was becoming rampant in the streets.

I have distinct memories, unpleasant memories, of this phase of the Depression. I remember in particular the so-called apple-sellers. They seemed to be on every corner, especially in the Wall Street area, with apples their only source of income.

These were the days before organized relief on a nationwide scale. Money was very tight and businesses and banks were failing along with the farmers. Such was the disorder in the country that organized crime functioned with pulverizing force. Ganglords such as Dutch Schultz and Lucky Luciano exerted a leadership more effective than that of the local and national governments.

The national budget, along with everybody else's, was out of kilter, and most of the new ideas for alleviating the public distress would increase public spending and aggravate the rate of inflation. There was tremendous concern about stimulating inflation, then as now, and this was justified. The needed skills of assessing real requirements and the political art of allotting priorities were scarcely even comprehended.

What was instantly clear, however, was that we all had to get into the fight against the Depression, and that might entail taking on new forms of public service. Averell went down to Washington the following year and was appointed Administrative Officer of the National Recovery Administration, the old blue-eagle NRA.

One morning, I happened to go to Washington on the day after the Supreme Court had declared the NRA to be unconstitutional. I went to a small apartment Averell kept at the Mayflower Hotel and sat down with him to breakfast. I asked, "How do you feel now that you're out of a job?" I had thought he might be feeling somewhat bitter. But Averell said he really didn't give a damn except he was leaving that afternoon for Montana, where he would receive a degree and had intended to give a speech about the NRA. "Now, I've got to throw that away and write a new one on the way out."

Averell, in fact, helped establish a tradition at Brown Brothers Harriman in which the firm willingly contributed its manpower and their leadership to the well-being of the country. I have told about how Bob Lovett became Assistant Secretary of War (Air) for Roosevelt and eventually Secretary of Defense for Harry Truman. During the Eisenhower years, Prescott Bush became United States senator from Connecticut. Pres was beaten the first time out by some three thousand votes out of a million cast. And the thing that swung the election against him was a statement in Drew Pearson's column, the day before the vote, that Pres was the treasurer of Planned Parenthood. It was too late to say that Pres was only treasurer of a theater benefit on behalf of Planned Parenthood in New York City. Connecticut had too many Catholic voters in those days to whom Planned Parenthood was anathema.

Two years afterward, Pres won hands down, and he made a great mark in the Senate. He was on the Banking Committee and other important committees, and he was honored and respected by his fellow senators. Pres was a born leader and we missed him in the firm, but we could spare him because we had very able young men who were coming along who were ready to play their parts. We honored Pres's desire to do something on behalf of the country, and he did it. He was a real asset to our nation.

It was during this ghastly Depression that I also became involved in public service. It began when three fellows decided it was not enough to worry about inflation, and that they should do something about it. One was Grenville Clark, a noted lawyer, and another was Archibald Roosevelt, the son of Theodore Roosevelt and a former classmate of mine, and the third man was Tom Barber. Just what he did, I never knew.

Well, they invited about two hundred of their acquaintances to a meeting one afternoon at the Harvard Club to discuss the affairs of the nation. This meeting I attended. They pointed out that the national budget had reached an unprecedented height of, whatever next, $4 billion. Today the national budget stands in excess of $300 billion, but in those days $4 billion seemed unconscionable.

Out of the $4 billion, it seemed that $1 billion went for debt service, interest and other things which nobody could do much about. A second billion went for defense, and no one would want to reduce that sum in the 1930s. A third billion went to finance the operations of all the government offices, agencies, bureaus, divisions and what have you. But the fourth billion was made up of benefits and pensions to veterans. Here was something that surely could be looked into.

They had found out that the system of veterans' benefits was unfair. Men who had been in the Army for perhaps a week who had never even left the country, but who had gotten into some accident or had been stricken with some illness, would qualify for the same benefits as men who had been wounded in battle.

Another charming little tidbit they discovered was that there were still twelve widows of veterans of the War of 1812 collecting widows' benefits. The War of 1812! Probably what had happened was that some young girls had gotten married to ninety-year-old veterans on their deathbeds, just so they could collect the pensions.

It was decided at the Harvard Club meeting that we should petition Congress for relief—which is one of the privileges extended by the Constitution. We agreed that the veterans' lobby was powerful and there would be little chance of success, but the tactic was worth trying.

We all signed the petition and Grenville and Archie went down to Washington to see President Hoover, who had just been defeated in the 1932 election but would remain in office until the following spring.

President Hoover put up the same argument. He said the veterans' lobby was far too powerful and nothing would come of our idea. But we persuaded Hoover it was worth a try.

So the last thing President Hoover did, the day before he ceased to be President, was to veto the Supplementary Appropriations Bill which contained the provision for the costly and unfair veterans' benefits and pensions. This threw the measure into the next Congress.

Next we put in a word with President Roosevelt through the Democratic National Chairman, Jim Farley, about the situation. We stressed to him that the veterans' benefits were consuming one fourth of the national budget. Under the established system, at the end of the next ten years, the veterans' benefits would cost not $1 billion, but $9.5 billion.

President Roosevelt was sufficiently impressed that in one of his first messages to Congress he called for an examination, review and alteration of the legislation concerning veterans' benefits and pensions. And the Congress, by gosh, stood up and did its job, and the veterans' benefits were streamlined, modernized and in sum reduced. The veterans who had been hurt in the fighting got more benefits. Those who had not been hurt got fewer benefits.

We were certainly jubilant about what we had accomplished, and I had never seen anything like it in my life. Just a handful of people had proven able to help change the course of financial matters in the federal government.

How much money did we save the country, the taxpayers, or both? Well, as I recall, the change in the law in President Roosevelt's first term reduced our spending on the veterans' benefits from $1 billion to something like $700 million. And, as I mentioned, if the earlier system had remained in effect, the top figure would not have been $1 billion, but $9.5 billion.

Today the idea that a small group of private citizens could go out and save 10 per cent of the national budget would be absolutely unbelievable.

But we did it—and my partners were proud of us, too.

The National Economy League, as we now called ourselves, was non-partisan and non-profit. We had a conglomeration of supporters, and this grew rapidly. Admiral Byrd of Antarctica fame was chairman and Henry Curran, a man long active in the political vineyards, was president. We had a hard-working management board and, after our success in veterans' benefits, we felt we could be of continued assistance. We stated in our literature that we intended to devote ourselves primarily to the reduction of wasteful and unjustifiable government expenditures—federal, state and local—and we meant it.

I had always believed in Mr. Micawber's celebrated economic dictum, that twenty pounds of income and nineteen pounds of expenses equaled happiness, while nineteen pounds of income and twenty pounds of expenditures equaled misery. And although it was difficult, if not impossible, to control income, it was possible to control expenditures. The one thing almost all of us have some control of is what we do with our money, such money as we get, and we can adjust our lives accordingly.

It seemed to me then, as it does now, that what is good for people is good for government, and that government can also adjust its expenditures with a sense of responsibility to the present and future generations. If it has a tidy treasury, then it is able to divert monies into special expenditures whenever emergencies arise. But all too often government spends more than it takes in to solve what appears to be a constant stream of emergencies. When it does this, then we are in a state of permanent emergency and permanent inflation.

Yes, I do agree with Micawber. His dictum is not fashionable these days, but I have seen one nation after another experience the disastrous effects of inflation, and one of the primary causes of inflation is loss of confidence in the management of the national treasury. That feeds right down the line.

The New Deal was predicated on a different economic theory, of course, that pump-priming expenditures would create income, and that the income side of the equation could be improved. Sometimes we do have to spend money to keep an emergency from growing to unmanageable proportions, and the Depression was surely an emergency.

There was a valid background for the concept that we should spend money to make money. But we cannot do it all the time, in too big a way, or so we thought in the National Economy League. Thrift still, from top to bottom, was a good watchword for the management of the funds with which we fought the Depression.

Although as a good Republican I would claim the Fifth Amendment if I was asked whether Roosevelt was a good President, I thought that some of the New Deal measures were better than others. But we concentrated on specific analysis, and the National Economy League bore down most strongly on taxation anomalies. For example, we proved able to trace the imposition of fifty-three separate taxes on every loaf of bread, and that is true today.

For example, we found six taxes being paid by farmers, such as:

1.) Real estate tax
2.) Sales tax on machinery
3.) Personal property tax on machinery and trucks
4.) Auto and truck state license tax
5.) State income tax
6.) Federal income tax.

Six more taxes of a similar nature were paid at the grain elevator level.

Five more taxes were being paid by the flour miller.

Eleven more taxes were being paid by the railroad that transported the product.

Seven more taxes were paid by the flour trucker.

They even got the bread wrapper manufacturer for seven more taxes.

And when the whole thing got to the baker, they put on eleven more taxes.

It seemed to all of us at the National Economy League, therefore, that every time we bit into a piece of bread, we were contributing to fifty-three separate taxes.

At this point, it would be fair to say that President Roosevelt, while still a candidate, had commented: "Taxes are paid in the sweat of every man who labors, because they are a burden on production and can be paid only by production. If excessive, they are reflected in idle factories, tax-sold farms, and hence, in the hordes of the hungry tramping the streets and seeking jobs in vain. There is not an unemployed man—there is not a struggling farmer—whose interest in this subject is not direct and vital."

But the New Deal, as it wore on, was driven increasingly by the insidious dictum, "Tax and tax, spend and spend, elect and elect."

Specifically, in the three fiscal years 1934, 1935 and 1936, the federal government spent almost as much money as the federal government had spent from the day George Washington took the oath of office.

How long the government could run in the red, and how much debt the nation could stand, were questions that bothered me deeply then, and still do now. Sooner or later the government and the people will have to face the blue music. Everybody knows that when money is borrowed, it has to be paid back.

This is the legacy which the present generation is passing on—and some, in some future time, might well wish that our present generation had never been born.

The National Economy League, of which I had become chairman, gradually learned that it had had its day. In veterans' benefits we had demonstrated a classic case of citizens' action to produce a more responsive government. In that sense, we were years ahead of our time. But the New Deal programs, some good, some bad, were blowing up the budget to the degree that our precise pinpricks could no longer make much difference. We attempted to arouse public opinion to demand tighter budgeting. But we were fighting against the times and we were not as effective in public relations as we had been in budget analysis.

We did have increasing pleasure in our association, and we had fun and saitsfaction, and we made a lot of new friends. We used to have dinners once a year, large public dinners, at which we raised money to help us keep going. I remember once that I volunteered to pay for the drinks at one of these affairs. For the first time in my life—and the last—I was stuck with a bill for drinks not by the drink but by the gallon.

Another story that signified, in an amusing way, one thing we were going through was told by Tom Barber, one of the founders of the League. Barber used to travel to different cities to drum up enthusiasm, and he used to ride in day coaches everywhere he went. He would talk to everybody who would listen, and vice versa. One day on the train in Kansas, an old farmer said that the daughters of the family now demanded all kinds of silk and satin for their underwear. "It's not like the old days.

I still remember many a time I'd read 'Pillsbury's Best' across Ma's ass."

During these middle years of my life I got involved in affairs in numerous other ways. For example, I was one of those rarest and least useful birds, a presidential elector.

It happened in 1928, and I was asked by my congressional district Republican leaders to be one of New York's electors for Herbert Hoover. On the appointed day, all the electors journeyed up to Albany to cast ballots for Hoover.

However, instead of taking ten or fifteen minutes, as we had assumed, the electoral procedure took all day. First we met, and we were prayed over, and then somebody made a speech. A lot more rinky-dink went on, and then we were all led over to the governor's office for a charming welcome by Franklin Roosevelt. Not until 4 P.M. did we get our chance to cast the ballots for President. And the ballots were not mere bits of paper on which we marked an X or a name. They were engraved cards, reading in effect, "I vote for Herbert Hoover." We saw them, we filed up and put them in a box and at last made a dash to catch the train back home.

There was only one benefit to Hoover's defeat four years later, as far as I could tell, and that was that I did not have to go through any more of that electoral foolishness. Of course, the electoral college is as dead as a dodo and something ought to be done to put it out of its misery. It is a waste of a lot of time and money for no purpose.

In the late 1930s, I took part in what I considered to be

a much more public-spirited enterprise, and that was an attempt to remove from office an isolationist congressman. I was against isolationism then as always, and it distressed me to see so many of our Republicans going down that road. Hamilton Fish represented my district, in Orange County, New York, and he had been in Congress for years and years. He was a very famous athlete, all-American football and all that. In fact, he was a prince of a fellow. But as his years in Congress had carried him along, he had become more and more of a menace to the thinking of some of us in the constituency. So when we saw the things happening that might involve us in the war in Europe, some of us decided to see if we could beat him.

Now it so happened that I had been interested for some time, from the investment standpoint, in what would now be termed the media. I had been one of the first investors in *Time* magazine in 1923. This was when Henry Luce and Briton Hadden were starting up. They had been a few classes behind us at Yale and they were financing by selling two or three thousand dollars' worth of stock to former Yale men, and I was one of these. Actually, the fairy godfather of *Time* was Edward H. Harkness, who loaned them a lot of money before they got the venture to a break-even point. The money I made on *Time* paid for a lot of bad investments I had previously made.

I had also been one of the investors in *Newsweek*. One of *Time*'s top editors had resigned to start up *Newsweek*, and a number of our friends backed him in a small way. Unfortunately, his estimates were wrong, and he went bust. About this time, Averell and Vincent Astor had started a somewhat similar magazine, with Raymond Moley as editor, entitled *Today*. We put *Newsweek* and *Today* together, and we bowed out. Vincent and Averell got Malcolm Muir to manage the new enterprise, and they put up the money. By golly, Malcolm Muir made a success of it. I came in on the tail end again. When Averell went to Washington, he had to divorce himself from *Newsweek* for fear of a conflict of interest. In his stead I served on the board of *Newsweek*, which was later sold to the Washington *Post* at a good profit to Vincent and Averell.

But our attempt to gain political influence through the media was not exercised at this national level. Our objective was to replace the isolationist congressman in our own home district.

One day, a man had come in to see me who said he was the publisher of a newspaper in Middletown, New York, which is about twenty-five miles from our home at Arden. He said he needed some financial help. I loaned him some money—and within a year I owned the paper. There was a competitor in town, another paper, and it was doing better than we were. So I went to the famous Frank Muncy, the publisher of the New York *Sun*, and asked him if he could help me find an editor. He could and did. He sent along a fine young man, who was a comer on a New York newspaper, a very attractive fellow who had never lived in the country and did not know how to run a country newspaper. This is an art in itself. I finally had to let him go, and we parted friends.

I was somewhat at a loss as to what to do with my newspaper when, lo and behold, an auditor asked me if he could have a go at it. He was an auditor who had been in one of our shipbuilding concerns, and I had asked him to keep an eye on the newspaper's finances. He told me, "I'd like to move to Middletown and I'd like to have a try at publishing the paper." I said, "Go ahead. Have a try." And it was this auditor who turned the newspaper around.

In the turn-around process, I had to buy the other newspaper in town, because there was not really enough room for two, and the whole thing began to go so well I began to have offers from newspaper chains. The accountant was Charlie Koons, long since dead, and nobody would have ever picked him out as a newspaperman. He made friends and got along well with people, he was quiet, and he was honest, and he rode herd on the editorial staff. He also hired an editor who was a sort of a firebrand and did not pull his punches.

Once I had to write a personal apology on the front page of the paper to the justices of the New York Supreme Court, because my editor had slandered them. I just groveled. I could not apologize enough. Two or three of the judges were my bosom friends at the racetrack, however, and the matter in hand has slipped my memory. I forgot what we said.

One of the difficulties in defeating Congressman Ham Fish was in finding a suitable Republican candidate. We finally found a young surrogate judge in nearby Newburgh, New York, a man named Bennett, a fine fellow, and we told him his future was made if he won. We threw the all-out support of the Middletown media behind Bennett in the Republican primary, but Fish was too strong.

The next time around, we put together an alliance with

the Democrats, and Bennett became our Democratic-Independent Republican candidate. This time we beat Ham Fish, and it was 1940, just before we became involved in World War II. Because of the length of his tenure in Congress, Fish could have chosen between the chairmanship of the Ways and Means Committee and the Foreign Affairs Committee.

Bennett served with distinction for two years and then what did Orange County do? It snowed him under because he had deigned to accept Democratic support. Or there might have been some general kind of apathy. I remember how we decided to have a rally in the county seat at Goshen. We advertised the rally, hired a band, and the candidate was ready to speak from the bandstand. But at the appointed hour, there were only fifty adults, two hundred youngsters and three hundred dogs on hand. On the way home I stopped off at the corner drugstore to buy a pack of cigarettes and there everybody was, lined up three deep, swilling Coca-Colas and strawberry sodas. I am afraid this is still the attitude of most people when it comes to politics.

As for the newspaper, when I got an offer from one of the chains, I said, "If you'll take the staff with you, it's for sale." Later, one of them agreed to take the staff, and I sold it, and we got back our investment with a nice profit.

In another area of my involvement in public affairs in the 1930s, I served as a member of the so-called "runaway grand jury" in 1935. This was the grand jury specially empaneled to look into the extremely serious situation with regard to organized crime in New York City. We were dealing with the rackets at first hand, and this was indeed a fascinating experience. We were just beginning to find out how much power the racketeers had built up over the years. They controlled whole industries. They controlled whole labor unions. They were obviously obtaining political protection at very high levels of the government, but we did not know how, nor from whom.

The grand jury, twenty-three of us, met in one of the government buildings on Lafayette Street. It was a room with a desk in front, and as I recall, the jurors sat in a semi-circle in two rows. The district attorney, William Copeland Dodge, or an assistant named Lyon Boston, or others, would produce witnesses and ask questions, and then we could ask questions. It was a tedious process, and we began to feel we were not getting the real story.

One day we did get the real story when Mayor La Guardia's commissioner of markets, William Fellowes Morgan, described a particularly vicious racket in the poultry industry. He said flatly that racketeers were obtaining protection from James J. Hines, then the Tammany Hall leader in the Eleventh District, a powerful ally of President Roosevelt's and the principal dispenser of federal patronage in New York City.

No single incident prompted our grand jury, however, to break away from the pattern in which we were being confined. It just grew on us that we were getting no place, and we more or less agreed among ourselves that something had to be done. We fortunately had an excellent foreman, Lee Thompson Smith, a splendid citizen and a fine man. He was the ringleader in our move to break away from the district attorney and go after crime on our own.

Late in the spring of 1935, our grand jury "ran away." We announced that we would hold our own hearings, call our own witnesses, take our own testimony and formulate our own conclusions. This was dynamite in the gangster-ridden city. We sat every day, including Saturdays, for three months, and we got tremendous support from the press and from reform-minded politicians of all parties. We even felt strong enough to exclude the district attorney and his assistant from our proceedings altogether. We felt sure this man had something to hide.

Finally, we decided that we would do what we had the right as grand jurors to do, and this was to petition the governor of New York to appoint a special prosecutor. We went up to Governor Herbert H. Lehman's house and we gave him a choice of several people who we thought would be good special prosecutors. One of the names on the list was that of Thomas E. Dewey, a young former United States Attorney who had obtained a spectacular conviction of the racketeer Waxey Gordon.

Governor Lehman, a Democrat not of the Tammany stripe, did not want to advance the Republican hopeful Tom Dewey, and he managed to stall the appointment for several days. Instead, he said he would make his choice from a group of four eminent jurists. But Lehman was scuppered when these four jurists declared in a unanimous statement that they would not take the job, and that Dewey should be appointed forthwith. Lehman had no choice but to make Dewey the special prosecutor of the rackets investigation.

Special Prosecutor Dewey made history in the months ahead with his convictions of Lucky Luciano, the Mafia leader, his hounding of the garment racketeers Lepke and Gurrah, and his shattering of a score of industrial rackets built upon hoodlum violence. He also obtained the conviction of Hines for political corruption. So our grand jury had launched Tom Dewey's restoration of public confidence in law enforcement, and this again was exciting public service in these Depression years.

Later I got to know Tom Dewey, not intimately, but well. He had moved to Tuxedo Park, not far from Arden. He lived summers in a rented house, and he used to commute on the train to the city. His life was in constant danger, and although he would chat and talk with us in the railroad car, he would never allow his friends to walk beside him when he got onto or off the train.

Dewey was as fine an administrator as he was a courageous person, and I think he made a good governor of New York and would have made a good President. I must say, in all fairness, however, that I think Harry Truman was one of the greatest Presidents our country has ever had.

How was I able to schedule this involvement in public affairs? The very simple reason is that I always had good partners. Always, when a venture into public affairs was involved, there were partners who were ready to fill in. I was working with people who could and did take over, who took care of things, and I am eternally grateful.

I would not like to leave the impression, however, that we always had the freedom of choice of what to get involved in and what not to get involved in in business and public affairs. Every so often there would be a crisis to which we were compelled to respond.

For example, my father had been a director of the Delaware and Hudson Railroad. This was a relatively small railroad that ran from the coal fields of eastern

Pennsylvania up through Binghamton, New York, to Albany, and thence to Canada. Coal was a principal form of energy and coal hauling was the principal business of the railroad.

Over the years, the Delaware and Hudson had been very profitable, and it was headed by a fascinating character, Leonor F. Loree, who was one of the last of the rugged individualists. He was a top-flight railroad man, and a top-flight doer of things on his own. He also was responsible and renowned for the founding of the Newcomen Society.

Well, things went along swimmingly through the late 1920s, and then new laws were passed requiring the railroad to separate itself from the coal-mining industry. There would have to be a railroad company and a coal company. After forming the coal company, Loree mortgaged it for a substantial amount and used the proceeds to buy control of the Wabash Railroad. He subsequently sold this railroad, without letting the directors know anything about it, to the Pennsylvania Railroad. Loree made a huge profit for the Delaware and Hudson.

Next, Lorre decided that there would have to be a realignment of the eastern railroads sooner or later, and it was important that Delaware and Hudson affiliate itself with the strongest and best. At that time, New York Central seemed to him to be the best bet, and so he bought a very substantial amount of New York Central stock, again without telling the directors of the Delaware and Hudson anything about it.

I had been a director of this railroad since 1921. At one board meeting in the late 1920s, I asked Loree in which securities the company's funds were invested. He politely but firmly told me to mind my own business. I was disturbed and told Averell, "I don't like this Delaware and Hudson business. I think I'll resign."

Averell said, "Don't do that. Something might happen." It sure did. The Depression hit the national economy and the railroad industry head on.

About that time, Loree became senile, literally incapacitated, and we had the traditional problem of what happens when a one-man band loses the one man. The rest of the management had been completely dominated by Loree, and lived by Loree's methods, and continued to withhold disclosures of consequence. By then the Delaware and Hudson seemed about ready to go into bankruptcy. Then they told the Board everything, and it was a real emergency.

The Board formed two committees as it took charge. One was an operations committee, of which I was chairman, and the other was a financial committee, of which Gates McGarrah, the banker, was chairman. We worked very closely together in pulling back expenditures and by a lot of hard work we were able to avoid bankruptcy. One day, we had liquid assets of $20,000, and we faced a payroll of scores of thousands of dollars, but we weathered it.

Next, we were fortunate enough to find a man by the name of Joseph Nuelle, a man with wide experience in both the railroad and the coal industries. We got Nuelle to take the reins. With Nuelle's contribution, and with the improvement in the economy we began to experience in 1937, we made it back.

Soon the D&H began to pay dividends again, but small ones, because too many people were converting from coal to oil to meet their energy requirements. The railroad rocked along in satisfactory shape and had another stroke of luck. It was just about the time Nuelle was ready to retire that William White, who had been president of the New York Central until he lost a proxy fight, was ready to take on a new assignment.

White walked upstairs to Nuelle's office—they were in the same building—and said, "I want a job. I want to be vice-president." Nuelle said, "No you won't. You'll be president. I'll be chairman of the Board and I'll retire in a year or so and you'll be in."

White made good progress until an individual came on spoiling for a fight. This man represented a large holding, held in an investment trust, which wanted to use the Delaware and Hudson as the nucleus of a New England railroad system.

By a lot of skillful handling, including a red-hot proxy fight, we were able to sell the Delaware and Hudson to the Norfolk and Western Railroad at a favorable price, and this left us with a sizable chunk of money in the treasury. Our friend with the big ambitions saw that there was a pot of gold. So we had another proxy fight with him, very close, too close for comfort, and we won out.

Finally, we put an end to what seemed like a constant succession of crises and emergencies in this property by selling it, together with the $60 million in the treasury, to one of the newly formed conglomerates. This was a rather fascinating conglomerate. The fellow who ran it had started out making pancakes in California. He formed a chain of pancake houses and branched off into this and that, and he was going great guns. The franchise business was booming then. And so we sold what was left of the Delaware and Hudson to this fellow in exchange for some prior securities of his.

All the other stockholders were enabled, through this tax-free exchange, to sell their stock in the pancake company at substantial profit. Now, that pancake company, like so many other conglomerates, has since had its troubles. But at least every Delaware and Hudson stockholder had the chance to get out with a profit.

It was an interesting situation, with lots of drama and excitement, and it was really touch and go. If the directors, including my partner, John Madden, whom we had induced to become chairman, had not worked hard during the ticklish moments, if they had not thoroughly lived up to their responsibilities to the stockholders, there might well have been a disaster.

CHAPTER VI: ONE WAY TO RUN A RAILROAD I

In an era in which distance is often measured not in miles but in light-years, it might have seemed odd when we celebrated the centennial anniversary of the driving of the golden spike at Promontory, Utah. It was May 10, 1969. And in an age in which we cross oceans and continents in a few hours, there are many who must find the inscription on the simple monument at Promontory a bit flowery. It reads:

"The last rail is laid! The last spike is driven! The Pacific Railroad is completed! The point of junction is 1,086 miles west of the Missouri River, and 690 east of Sacramento City."

Viewed by today's standards, however, the message Leland Stanford and T. C. Durant telegraphed to the White House and to all the waiting nation was modest indeed. A mere 1,776 miles of railroad track! Little indeed to Space Age pioneers. Yet a generation of pioneers who had built their new homes and new lives in the western wilderness reflected on those long miles often and often sadly. Having trudged across the mountains, prairies and deserts of the continent, they had been removed effectively from the two coasts.

How important was the construction of our first transcontinental railroad to the development of the United States! How right they were, those prophets of the iron horse, and how correctly the railroad builders envisaged and foresaw the needs of their neighbors to span those awesome miles. How correctly they judged the economic, political and social miracles that would follow the rails.

Since the driving of the golden spike at Promontory, in which the Union Pacific and the Central Pacific celebrated their juncture, the transcontinental railroads have indeed made possible the carving out of a great empire in the American West. Five times since the golden spike, during three full-scale wars and two undeclared armed conflicts, the railroads carried the military by the millions, plus the mountains of their weapons and equipment, another service foreseen by the builders of the initial transcontinental route. The railroad miles became efficient miles, easy miles, miles that made life more enjoyable and more profitable, in the best sense, throughout the American West, and in turn enriched the American East with treasure from mines, forests and agricultural development.

The engineers who surveyed the West for those first rail lines, the builders who laid the first rails and ties, the men who put up the money, the operators of the first amazing trains, they too made possible the later mapping and construction of the highways and freeways that crisscross the nation—even though an integrated transportation system still seems to be beyond our grasp.

Less than thirty years after the golden spike, however, the Union Pacific had survived successive scandals only to confront a general bankruptcy. It was in the mid-1890s that my father moved to save the Union Pacific. Together with Kuhn Loeb & Co., he presented a plan to reorganize the railroad and he won acceptance of it, becoming a member of the new Board of Directors. Within a very short time, a matter of months, he became president. He supposedly once remarked, "All I need is to be a member of the executive committee."

It was typical of him that the first thing he did with the railroad was to tour it, with his business car plumped backward in front of the engine so that he could view every bit of the two streaks of rust across the prairies and the mountains.

I understand that, during this first trip, he telegraphed Kuhn Loeb that he needed immediately $25 million to begin the rehabilitation of the line. This he obtained, and he set about establishing what came to be known as the Harriman standards of construction for modern railroads. His whole belief was that in order for any property to do its job, to perform a service and to make a profit, that property had to be in good physical shape, in a state of good maintenance and repair.

Well, much has been written about the fact that the two streaks of rust were rebuilt into a modern railroad in an unbelievably brief period of months, and the whole secret of Union Pacific has been the maintenance of that position ever since. Huge amounts of money have been invested in improving the roadbed, reducing the curva-

ture, modifying the gradients, tunneling through mountains, all for the purpose of enabling more powerful
trains to move faster with heavier loads.

Yes, the Union Pacific—how to comment on something
that has been a part and parcel of my life as long as I
remember?

I can remember traveling across the continent at night,
a boy in one of those early trains. There was naturally no
air conditioning, and we had to pull up the windows to
let the air in, and we had to keep the screens on to keep
the flying cinders out. I used to lie in bed on the trains
and stay awake just to listen to the whistle as we went by
crossings and other places. It was fascinating, romantic
to me.

I remember the last railroad trip I took with my father,
not too long before he died. He had a special train made
up of what were called "business cars." These were not
the "private cars" that rich people used to ride in, those
luxurious, fabulous relics of yesteryear. My father's business cars were what we would call mobile offices. When
he was away, his business cars were his office and his
home.

On this particular trip, we must have had all the Union
Pacific brass on board, because there were about eight or
ten business cars. There might have been some Southern
Pacific men on board, too, because my father by now
had won control of the Southern Pacific as well. And on
the first day out, my father told me, "Roland, you're the
commissary general." I was eleven years old, and he was
putting me in charge of arranging the meals for the executives, ordering the food, deciding which cars people
would eat in, working out with him whatever sort of

seating plans he needed so that all the executives would not sit in the same place at each meal.

I used to love to ride up front in the locomotive, needless to say, and I always had to come back and take a bath before doing anything else. I am afraid that the something else often had to be the boring lunches and dinners at the places we would stop at. I used to get awfully sleepy while my father and his associates conversed with the local leaders about the growth and development of their city, township or state.

Only about ten or fifteen years ago I was attending a meeting of the Old Timers' Club, an organization of Union Pacific men active or retired who have worked on the railroad for twenty-five years. I used to renew my friendships at these affairs with a lot of the men I had known in the old days. One man came up and said hello. He said, "You don't have the slightest recollection of me, but I sure remember you." He reminded me of the opening of one of my father's most notable achievements, the Lucin cutoff built across the Great Salt Lake itself. "I was the brakeman on the train," the old-timer said. "You were left in my charge—and you could ask the damnedest questions."

One evening, after hunting in the forests and mountains, a half-dozen friends and I got stranded in West Yellowstone, Montana. We looked like a bunch of bums, and none of us had any money. So I went to the station agent and said, "I'm Roland Harriman." I explained the situation to him and asked for some money to tide us over the night. He said, "How do I know you're Roland Harriman?" I said I had no identification and he would have to take my word for it.

The station agent then declined to advance me any money, but he said, "You go over to that hotel over there, and I'll stand you for supper, bed and breakfast, and I hope it turns out all right."

I said, "It's a long time until supper. Can't you give us just a little spending money?"

He said, "All right, here's fifty cents," and we had a high old time with this.

At another Old Timers' meeting, this man came up to me and said, "You remember the time when someone staked you at West Yellowstone?" I said, "I sure do." He said, "I'm the guy."

After my father died, Judge Lovett carried on the Harriman tradition. I was elected a member of the Board of Directors in 1921 and I have served in that capacity ever since. Over the years, I learned the railroad business and grew to know the people who operated the Union Pacific. I became knowledgeable gradually, very gradually, and also very thoroughly.

The 1920s were dark days for the railroads as more and more restrictions and regulations were placed upon us by government authority. Not so many new people came into the business, which was a shame, because we would be needing them in the 1930s and the 1940s. Then came the Great Crash and the subsequent business decline. The Union Pacific business seemed to begin to evaporate, and we were seriously considering cutting the dividend and preparing for storm conditions. Suddenly, lo and behold, we struck oil on our property in Wilmington, California, a suburb of Los Angeles.

At this point, I would like to make it clear that one

reason the Union Pacific was supposed to have been so profitable was that it had received large land grants from the government during the construction of the lines. What most people did not know, however, was that the government got its money's worth many times over because of the stipulation that the railroad would serve the government at half price for freight and passengers.

This arrangement lasted until the late 1940s, after the massive military transports of World War II. By then, the Union Pacific had paid back to the government in reduced fares and rates many times the value of the land it had been given.

Most people also do not realize that most of the oil strikes made by the Union Pacific were not on government grant land. These were made on properties that the Union Pacific had acquired at its own expense. The Wilmington field, for example, was on land that had been bought by the Union Pacific as a likely center for industrial development.

Of the land grant land, much was sold off by the railroad in the early days at very low prices to encourage settlers to move in. This was part and parcel of the building of the American West to which I have referred. What is now left of the land grant land for the Union Pacific is largely sagebrush and lava rock country. It is true that, on some of it, there have been important discoveries of metals and minerals, but not oil, to any great extent.

So, the discovery of the Wilmington oil field rescued the Union Pacific dividends in the 1930s. Then came World War II, and business boomed. But the excess taxes were high during this period also, and our ability to maintain our properties was diminished by the nationwide shortages of labor and materials. So we had to spend at the end of the war about as much as had been spent on the original line, just to get our operations back into shape. But this is jumping ahead a bit.

There were many fine people I knew during my early years as a director of Union Pacific. There was our president, Carl R. Gray, a very fine gentleman indeed. The only time I found him off base was once when I had expected to meet him in Omaha on my way east, and he sent me a wire from Chicago, "VERY SORRY, CANNOT MEET YOU, AM DETAINED IN CHICAGO." Of course, I knew the next morning when I opened the paper what had detained him. It was the Dempsey-Tunney fight.

An astonishing character succeeded Gray, a man by the name of Bill Jeffers. Here was an extraordinary fellow, who had come up through the ranks of the railroad industry, literally from water boy to president. He was the czar of the railroad. He ran it himself. If there was an accident, he soon would be on the scene in person. If a yard got tied up for some reason or another, he would be there to find out why.

Jeffers was fond of a story about my father, who had once asked a lieutenant to go out and inspect a railroad property and submit a report. When the man said it would take at least a week to finish the report, my father sent back word, "I want it today by telegraph."

Bill Jeffers also expected miracles from his subordinates, and if he did not get the miracles he would fire the subordinates. I am not exaggerating. Bill often regretted his hasty dismissals and would ask the men to come back. At one time, the executive committee was

124

busy rehiring at Bill's recommendation the very executives he had fired the week before.

I remember one famous story about Bill Jeffers. There was a road gang down in the Nevada desert, in the middle of the summer. Every road gang literally had to report progress to Jeffers every day. Well, the foreman admitted one day that they had laid off work, because the temperature had risen to more than 120 degrees in the shade. Jeffers wired, "What are you doing in the shade?"

Well, in spite of it all, he had a great character, and he really made things hum.

After his retirement from the Union Pacific, he moved to Los Angeles, where he was promptly tapped by the mayor to be the czar against smog. I should have mentioned that Bill had also been made czar of the rubber industry during a period of wartime shortages. But the smog was too much for Jeffers, and it is still there.

The Union Pacific retained Jeffers as a consultant after his retirement, and he used to represent us sometimes at meetings with shippers. I got a complaint from him. He wired me, "I went to a meeting of shippers. The Southern Pacific had ten men there. The Santa Fe had twelve men there, and I was the only man representing Union Pacific. What's wrong with our Traffic Department?" I wired back, "Bill, since when isn't one Jeffers equal to ten Southern Pacific and twelve Santa Fe men?"

One place Bill Jeffers did make a mistake was in his recommendation of his successor as president. This was a man named Ashby, a very experienced fellow who had come up through the Accounting Department. Ashby left for personal reasons, to be replaced by Art Stoddard, another who had come up through the ranks of railroading, but who had also assimilated some knowledge of the oil industry. Stoddard was a very useful man until his health failed and he had to retire. This opened the door to Edd Bailey, a real crackerjack in every way, a great railroad man, a great guy, again with the old come-up-through-the-ranks experience. But once again I am jumping ahead.

What I am jumping ahead of is my brother Averell, who served in the 1930s as chairman of the Board of Directors. He somehow managed to fit this in between and around his stints in government, until in 1946 he was appointed to Cabinet rank as Secretary of Commerce. Then, to avoid any conflict of interest, he resigned as chairman and I succeeded him.

Averell, in the 1930s, decided that a serious attempt ought to be made to modernize and even glamorize our passenger service in order to make it more competitive. We ran second sections on fast trains composed entirely of coaches. We improved the comfort of the coach cars, installing reclining seats, and we served good, inexpensive snack meals.

As a matter of fact, we were proud of our passenger service and this was an important part of our enterprise. During the war we were so crowded with troops and regular passengers that we served only two meals a day in the dining cars. We started serving breakfast at 5 A.M., and we would not get through breakfast until noon. Then we would have to clean up, prepare the next go-round and open the car again at 3 P.M. for dinner, which would be served until 9 P.M.

This was passenger service with a vengeance for us because, as Bob Lovett once calculated, it would have been cheaper for us to pay everybody who did not eat in the dining car the sum of two dollars than to continue to supply the service. But one year during the war we actually came within $25,000 of breaking even on the dining cars.

There would be much more to consider in the matter of passenger service on the Union Pacific and on all United States railroads, but this should not obscure the story of what had been accomplished in the past. I remember that one evening in 1950 I gave a dinner party for one of our senior executives on the occasion of his seventieth birthday and fifty years with the Union Pacific. I had asked the Union Pacific Museum at Omaha to send me some appropriate items from their collection. I remember that one of these was a passenger train schedule of approximately 1900.

The booklet was nearly half an inch thick, and each train was listed on a separate page, with the times of arrival and departure at all of the junction points meticulously and formally listed. A far greater number of pages was devoted to a list of towns and cities on the Union Pacific that boasted an opera house. Before the days of movies and television, or radio and other mass entertainment, the vaudeville and opera companies used to go from place to place by rail. They needed to know where they had proper facilities for putting on a show.

That was one example of the lengths to which the railroads went to drum up passenger travel. Of course, in the old days we also gave special rates for immigrants who were coming to settle in the West. We had immigrant railroad trains as well. The railroads had agents all over Europe who kept busy selling potential immigrants

on the glories of the American West, and the glories of
the Union Pacific as the best way to get there.

The Union Pacific was always well known for the ex-
cellence of its steam locomotives. We had a very fine en-
gineering department, and we developed steam power
that grew stronger and stronger. In the late 1930s, the
diesel engine began to be talked about in terms of locomotive power. Of course, diesels had been used in marine
and other engines for years. However, our then president,
Jeffers, decided that we should build the most powerful
steam locomotive in the world, and this is what he proceeded to do. He built what was famously known as the
"Big Boy."

The Big Boy was a colossal success—and Lord knows
how many millions and millions of tons of freight the
huge locomotive hauled during World War II. We built
about twenty-five of them, and after their distinguished
service, they were retired for the adulation of countless
railroad buffs and historians. Most were scrapped, but
one I know about stands in its glory in Cheyenne, Wyoming, and another in a railroad museum at Green Bay,
Wisconsin, a town famous for its football team and also
for its railroad museum. This museum has the locomotive and two cars that General Eisenhower used for his
headquarters when he was in England, and also two of
Winston Churchill's cars used during the war. And there
is also a Union Pacific Big Boy, which was itself a splendid war veteran in every respect.

Shortly after I became chairman of the Union Pacific
Board of Directors, and this was in 1946, the question of
dieselization assumed top priority. Our then president,

Ashby, was sold on the idea. He asked me into a meeting with a representative of the General Motors outfit that made the diesel engine. Then Ashby began to tell me all about the benefits of diesels to such an extent that I finally turned to the General Motors man and asked, "Who's the salesman around here?"

Well, we did start to use diesels and their superiority even over the Big Boy in economy of operation and dependability was so outstanding that, in one fell swoop, we decided to dieselize.

It is claimed, and I think quite rightly so, that electrification is the least costly way to power railroad operations, and we have been studying that for a long time, and maybe some one of these days, the Union Pacific will be electrified.

Now, I want to make it clear that the position of chairman under the Union Pacific bylaws in my day was not that of a so-called line officer. He was the go-between, between the Board of Directors, who create policy, and the operating people, who run the railroad. I found myself with very considerable responsibility for our planned postwar expenditures of approximately $455 million. This was more than the original railroad had cost to build.

We committed a large portion for dieselization, and there were also line changes. We built a new route over the Rocky Mountains from Cheyenne to Laramie, Wyoming. The new line is ten miles longer than the old, but the grades are much better, and the performance was improved at no cost whatever in time. We installed heavier rail—and one big development was not only in locomotive power but in the quality of our rolling stock. A freight car now holds twice as much as one did forty or fifty years ago. We have self-unloading coal cars, self-un-loading wheat cars and sometimes cars for special purposes, such as the transportation of automobile engines for automobile manufacturers.

The trouble was and is, as with everything else, that prices were increasing astronomically. Fifty years ago a boxcar might cost $800, but now they cost something like $18,000 to $25,000.

Anyway, we progress here, and progress there, and we compensate back and forth, but our power will now haul a hundred and fifty of today's modern cars up- and downhill—and remember that the Union Pacific is all up- and downhill, real hills. We developed all sorts of funny things—head engines, for example, in the lead; we would also put a couple of them in the middle of the train, and a couple at the rear, all of them controlled from the lead cab. We have radio control, from dispatchers to engineers, and the conductor in the caboose can talk to the engine.

We thought the Union Pacific Board of Directors ought to be made much more familiar with the operations of the line, and so we inaugurated some fairly intensive inspection trips. There were several informal directors' inspections, and some formal ones. I remember one of the informal ones that was rather amusing. About four of the directors and a couple of officers, including our general counsel, made up our party. We would stop off for lunch at some town with the local Chamber of Commerce to reacquaint ourselves with one another, and then we would ride on for dinner in the next town, with the next Chamber of Commerce.

At these meetings I would get up and talk briefly and

each of my trained seals, as I called the others, would make a short presentation. But our general counsel, Joe Mann, took a different tack. He had a great fund of funny stories, and there was one in particular that was rewarded by great laughter, so much so that he repeated this story every place we stopped.

Needless to say, the rest of the Union Pacific team grew less and less enchanted by Joe Mann's story. By threat and persuasion we tried to get him to tell another one. But the local applause was too much for this trained seal. He persisted, and I decided that some rugged form of action would have to be taken.

It was in Salt Lake City that I proclaimed the moment of truth. I called on one of the directors to talk ahead of Joe Mann, and, as arranged, he told Joe's story, and sat down. Then I promptly called on Joe. For the first time in his life Joe was absolutely at a loss for words. We had gotten even.

These trips were indeed very successful. I have always believed that Boards of Directors who are responsible for policy should know what management is talking about, and we gave ours a very thorough course indeed.

This reminds me of a strange characteristic of the railroad business, and it creates some difficulty in getting directors we want. Under the law, which was written in the days when too much cheating was indulged in by a few, no director of a railroad can own a substantial amount of stock in a company that sells supplies to the railroad. The word "substantial" has never been adjudicated. So our Union Pacific lawyers have ruled that "substantial" is an amount that would seem to be substantial to a juror in Kansas. In spite of these and other difficulties, we have been fortunate in the quality of the men who sit on our Board of Directors.

And here, once again, I want to bring up the name of Bob Lovett. From 1940 until 1953 he had served, off and on—mostly on—in important government positions. With the end of Truman's term, Bob came home for keeps in 1953. This was in the nick of time for us because just about then, Woody Charske, the chairman of our executive committee, died after more than fifty years of service. He was almost that "irreplaceable man."

Happily Bob Lovett agreed to take on the chairmanship of the executive committee. From that moment until our joint retirement from our official posts in 1969 we worked not as a team but as one man. We made decisions jointly if we were both available. If not, one of us would decide for both.

We two still serve on the Board and as members of the executive committee.

CHAPTER VII: ONE WAY TO RUN A RAILROAD II

All my life in the Union Pacific, in fact, I have loved the feel and the views of the country. It is true that the railroads were built where the grades were as easy as possible. This meant that we traveled through flat country wherever and whenever we could. The Denver and Rio Grande, for example, is renowned for its scenery in the midst of the Rockies, and some think the Union Pacific scenery is tedious by contrast. However, it is not tedious in the least if you are interested in how people live. Even in the prairies of Nebraska, for example, I have been always impressed by the massive expanses of grain and corn. I never cease to wonder at the precision with which the rows of corn are planted.

There was and there is a great feeling of depth to this country—a real basic value, of miles and miles and miles of crops. Of course, these are interspersed with great sagebrush flats, but these too will eventually be developed to handle the increase in our population. This is fertile land, a good part of it, but it needs water. Now whether we can find enough water to irrigate the so-called desert lands, our future generations will have to find out.

I do not think there is any danger that we might lose our sense of nationhood, even with our dizzying ability to fly from coast to coast and put in a reasonable working day or night at the other end. This sense of nationhood is something people who have never traveled across the continent by train, or even by automobile, can scarcely comprehend. There is a great deal of depth in the so-called wide-open spaces, and there is increasingly depth in population.

The townships in the prairies, the mountains and the deserts are scattered, yes, but they are growing along with the so-called megalopolises on the eastern and western coasts, not as rapidly perhaps, but they are filling up.

I was very much impressed in this regard when I served on the mortgage committee of an insurance company of which I was a director. Time after time, whenever a farm mortgage was being considered, a great point was made of the fact that the farm was being operated by the father and his sons, and in some cases by the father, sons and grandsons. It encourages me to think there are still families who believe in farming. It struck me that the day of the farmers is still a very long way from being over.

Of course, east, west and center, the farmers are being squeezed by the demand for building sites. And it does worry me to this extent, that the values of farm properties are rising so fast that the inheritance taxes are becoming almost unpayable. Most farm families are compelled, therefore, to sell.

On the other hand, it has always impressed me in the

so-called wide-open spaces that there is a tremendous growth in educational facilities. In a town some fifty or sixty miles south of our family ranch in Idaho, and that is a fairly wide-open space, there is a small, independent college. Ten, fifteen years ago, the enrollment in that little college used to be numbered in the hundreds. Now it is numbered in the upper four figures.

People there are striving for better education, and they are getting it, and the impact on the future of the region will be incalculable. At the present time, whether they can make full use of this more advanced education is doubtful. For instance, I was informed not long ago, and I believe it is true, that 50 per cent of the train crews of the Union Pacific in the 1960s, in the Kansas Division, were college graduates. I asked why young people with that kind of education were working as trainmen. I was told that the pay on the Union Pacific was better than anything else available in that region. All this is encouraging to me, and this is happening so much in what are still called the wide-open spaces.

In the Union Pacific land, we began to find some more oil and we found other minerals. It seemed apparent to us in the 1950s that no one man could run a railroad and an oil and mineral operation, not to mention a land business. So we began to make plans to divide the properties into logical segments. It took us a long time to achieve this, for complex financial reasons, but we did it. We got the railroad run by railroad men. We bought the Champlin Petroleum Company and it took over all our oil properties, so our oil operations are now being run by oil people. We formed a minerals company and put it in charge of

135

mineral operators. In the same way, we set up a land company to handle our land development.

For a railroad, of course, it is very important that new business be located on its property so that shipments may be maintained and expanded. We learned how to buy land, how to develop it sagaciously, how to put in streets, sewers and water lines, how to build new homes.

I would want to make clear that the Union Pacific Corporation, which became the holding body of all the above companies, was not, and is not, a conglomerate. The word "conglomerate" can have rather a shady meaning in many places, and we have been referred to as a conglomerate simply because our operations are so widespread. But we simply divided the functions of our existing business into logical components and that will be one secret, I am sure, of our continued success.

At the moment, we know where the oil is, we know where the coal is, we know where the trona is, we are hoping to find out where the uranium is, and maybe we will have some strange minerals that will be valuable in the future. For instance, twenty years ago, nobody had ever heard of trona. I never had. It used to be made artificially. They never called it trona, but soda ash. Soda ash is used in the manufacture of glass, paints and many other commercial processes and products. Nobody had ever heard of trona, and suddenly in the middle of the century, the Union Pacific found it had the largest deposits of trona in the world.

For starters, I think in the early 1950s, we leased the land where the trona had been located on a royalty basis. Soon we concluded this was a rather stupid thing to do, and when more and more demands came in for trona, we

GFH
1945

5. Gladys in wartime Red Cross uniform.

6. (*Following page*) "New" Arden Homestead about 1965.

7. Gladys and the author with companions at Arden Homestead about 1943.

8. Averell and the author about 1954.

joined forces with the Stauffer Chemical Company to build a plant at the minehead. This is near Green River, Wyoming.

All of our land has been well prospected and I do not think we will find any great amount of precious minerals. But you never know. For a number of years, our Oil Department and another oil company had been prospecting unsuccessfully for oil near Green River. Lo and behold, Champlin found a major new field nearby. It is always mystifying, a bit like drilling for water. You can drill for water and get a dry hole, and go ten feet over and find an artesian well.

Even historically, we never know. For example, coal used to be a very important part of the Union Pacific holdings. We used to mine it for use in our locomotives. When we converted to diesels, most of these coal properties were closed down. But even before the energy crisis we thought that coal would come back into its own, either in its own form or gasified or liquefied, or some other form. So we joined with a couple of groups, and we are conducting our own experiments in the use of coal.

It will take some time for us to redevelop our mines, to open some of them up again and start others. There are not sufficient cars around nowadays to move the vast tonnages of coal we would need to replace even partially fuel oil and natural gas. But the time is coming.

Neither are we confining our explorations to the continental United States. We have confirmed the discovery of a major oil field in the British North Sea, and we are conducting exploration in Peru and the Philippines and in the Gulf of Mexico.

The Union Pacific puts its bets on places where people

live or are going to live, in the same spirit in which we invest in geological considerations. One look at the map of the Union Pacific system, with its connections from Omaha and Kansas City to Los Angeles, to Portland, Seattle and Spokane, will disclose the booming metropolis that is the city of Denver, Colorado. There is tremendous growth around Denver and we have a lot of sites there, a lot of industrial development sites, and we have bet a great deal on the future of this city. We helped to develop it over decades, and now we are helping in its further expansion to meet what its people sometimes call its destiny.

Similarly, the Union Pacific pioneered in the development of Kansas City, Kansas, across the river from Kansas City, Missouri. It is the same thing with Topeka, Kansas, Cheyenne, Wyoming, and Omaha, of course, and then there are Pocatello and Boise, Idaho, all of them growing communities. There is not a place I can think of in which we are not of crucial importance in growth. There is also not a place I can think of today where our Land Division is not extremely active, keeping up the Union Pacific momentum.

Then there was Sun Valley, Idaho, and that was one of Averell's inspirations. Even before the war, people were becoming interested in skiing and in probing into beautiful mountain scenery and so on. Averell thought there were enough people who wanted to ski, so he hired an Austrian nobleman to come over and find a place on the Union Pacific system that could be made into a ski resort. This would be one way to build up the passenger service, too, to run all the new skiers to the new pleasure resort.

But the Austrian did not find any place that leaped to his attention on our system, and he became very discouraged.

Perhaps a bit belatedly, the Austrian then had the brilliant idea of examining the weather reports, and he soon found that Sun Valley was a place that had snow from December to April and a constant supply of almost everything else. This was at the far end of a far branch of the Union Pacific, but it was good enough.

The year Sun Valley opened, there was a great fanfare, and it did not snow for two weeks. Nothing like that had happened in most people's memories. Everybody had arrived for a skiing Christmas, and we had to feed them and sleep them for free, because there was none of the promised snow. It finally snowed on the last day of the year.

Sun Valley started booming pretty soon after that, as we all know, and this was partly due to a public relations man named Steve Hannagan, who had the idea of selling the place to movie people, and soon we were on the map. We built the lodge, and it was comfortable, and it became so popular that we decided to build the inn, which was less expensive, less posh, with four people in a room for dormitory-style ski vacations.

Sun Valley was a success for us, even though we did not profit from it directly, because it made people talk about and travel by the Union Pacific. This was what we had wanted. As rail passenger traffic kept sinking lower and lower, we eventually sold it to the Janss Brothers of Los Angeles in the mid-1960s. They did with it what we did not want to do. They went in big into real estate, and I think they made a good thing of it financially, and they are certainly changing the landscape.

The prime management policy we have had was that in

good years we prepared for the bad years, because there were always ups and downs. During the 1950s, other railroads began to get into serious trouble, and they kept going down and down. This did not happen to the Union Pacific, nor was it about to.

Much of the trouble, or shakeout if you like, resulted from the fact that too many railroads had been built in the latter part of the nineteenth century that did not justify their existence. The railroads in the Middle West, in particular, are a canful of worms, and there is said to be no farm in the state of Iowa that is more than twelve miles from a railroad. Nowadays, whenever anybody tries to close down even a small section of a railroad as redundant, there is an uproar from the politicians, who think the people will be hurt if something is taken away which they never use.

I remember one hearing, not for the Union Pacific, but the Delaware and Hudson. The Delaware and Hudson wanted to close down the passenger service on a little branch line, and they had to have hearings about it. On the day, there were about three hundred people jammed into the hearing room, all of them ready to protest vehemently against the cutting of railroad service.

Finally, the judge in charge of the hearings asked the crowd, "How many of you came here by train?" There was not one! "How many of you used this particular train in the last year?" There was not one! Small wonder that in this case the cutoff of this train was approved. There are many other reductions in service that ought to be granted in the country. Then the railroads would be able to spend the released money to improve the services that are really needed.

I remember talking with a man who had been building passenger airplanes in great numbers after World War II. He told me, "Well, we're going to take 95 per cent of your business during the next five years." I replied, "I know it, but please, while you're about it, take 100 per cent."

During these years, while passenger business continued to decline but freight business turned around and headed upward, some railroads were criticized for deliberately making their passenger service unpleasant and uncomfortable. There were notorious examples of this in and around our great cities. But even in terms of our unprofitable passenger business, I can say that the Union Pacific went down fighting. We determined that any passengers who wanted to travel on our trains would receive first-class equipment and first-class service. We had been fortunate in developing a lightweight, so-called streamlined train. This all started in the 1930s when Bob Lovett had brought some drawings back from Germany and Averell had fallen right in with the idea, and the Union Pacific developed our country's first lightweight, high-speed dieselized passenger train.

For a while, this helped bring back a few passengers, and we continued as late as the early 1960s to build new equipment. We reduced the time schedules of our trains, and we invested in good food, comfort and service. But it was a hopeless task.

In the end, the losses in the passenger business became a very serious matter, and along with the other railroads we welcomed the formation of Amtrak, the government-run passenger system. It is noteworthy that Amtrak got its best equipment from the Union Pacific and the Santa Fe.

There are still people who prefer to travel by train, and I think Amtrak is doing a pretty good job.

In fact, the Union Pacific hauls the San Francisco-bound Amtrak train from Denver to Ogden, Utah, on a three-times-a-week basis. I am glad to say that the best on-time record on all the Amtrak trains is for the run between Denver and Ogden.

With the energy crisis, and with the prospects of continuing shortages, not to mention the discomfort of other modes of travel, there is a chance that railroad passenger traffic will increase. Already the energy crunch has resulted in increased passenger travel on the commuter lines.

I might just as well mention a matter which has disturbed me for many years, of which I have spoken at great length, and to no avail. The commuter lines, so-called, of which fortunately the Union Pacific has none, are really an extension of metropolitan transport systems, subways, bus lines and so on. If, twenty or thirty years ago, the government had taken over the commuter lines —Lord knows I am against government ownership of railroads, but commuter lines, the extensions of the metropolitan systems, if the government had taken them over years ago—and if the government had spent on their rehabilitation, proper roadbed, proper equipment, one tenth of the amounts they have spent on building superduper highways and quickways in and out of cities, then we would not have the trouble we have right now.

Every highway that was built to take care of commuter automobile business was obsolete the day it opened. It just compounded the problem. But if comfortable, dependable commuter service had been provided, people would have used the railroads and we would not have all the automobiles dashing—not dashing, creeping—in and out of metropolitan centers daily. It would also have cost us much less than what we will now have to spend to clean up the mess.

The smog is just one horrendous thing that has been created by the slow-moving, gas-burning automobile engines. It just makes no sense at all.

Many people are going back to the use of mass transportation, and an effort is being made, and monies are being allocated by the government. At long last, they have awakened to the horrible mistake that was made.

When our corporate reorganization plans finally jelled, we all realized that we were fortunate to have in our organization a lawyer by the name of Frank Barnett. He had been chief counsel for the company, and he became chairman of the Board of the Union Pacific Corporation although they retained me as honorary chairman. This was in 1969. We also needed to have a president, with general, rounded-out business experience, to supervise our different operations. Again, we were fortunate enough to have on our Board of Directors such a man, James H. Evans, and we persuaded him to leave his then connection as head of a savings bank and to become president of the corporation. Likewise, we had in our ranks, as a director of long standing, Elbridge Gerry. His knowledge of our properties, together with his general business wisdom, made him our ideal balance wheel, so he was made chairman of the corporation's executive committee.

We enlarged the roster of corporate officers with some top-flight men from other companies, comptrollers, treasurers and so on. Remember, this was now the parent corporation, not the railroad company, nor the oil company, nor the mineral company, nor the land company, which were all run by men with years of experience in their fields.

We were particularly fortunate in finding for the presidency of the Union Pacific Railroad Company a man who had started his career on the Union Pacific. He took jobs with other railroads and then came back to us. And John C. Kenefick is one of the great leaders in United States railroading, perhaps the best there is today.

So, all in all, we developed a good organization, and although we had approved the Amtrak system for passenger service, we intended to avert the threat of nationalization of all the railroads per se. This is still talked about, although legislators and others we have attempted to educate do not realize that the losses on nationalized railroads elsewhere in the world are fantastically high.

Everybody talks about the high-speed Japanese trains, and it is true they are wonderful trains. But I am glad we do not all have to pay the Japanese tax rates to support them. The Canadian Pacific Railroad, privately owned, does pretty well financially, while the Canadian National Railroad, which is government-owned, is a financial flop.

In any event, the Union Pacific Corporation, by separating its other properties from the railroad operations, has made sure of one thing. If some ill-advised government does nationalize the railroads, they will not get the real estate, the oil fields, the minerals, not even the trona that we have brought along.

Now, the corporation's directors are also the directors of the railroad company. The chairman of the Board of the corporation is also the chairman of the Board of the railroad company. But the president of the corporation is not the president of the railroad company. All the authority comes up to and down from the corporation.

Frank Barnett, our chairman, recently was responsible almost entirely for the creation of a promising instrument for straightening out the mess of the northeastern railroads. We have no direct financial interest in the northeastern railroads, but it is important that we have good, viable connections. Penn Central, in particular, is the eastern end of much of our transcontinental freight business. So the Board permitted Frank and our present general counsel to spend some time to develop a plan. Without getting into arcane matters, Frank proved able to get the proper people in Congress to sponsor something that we all hope will work.

Three of the partners of Brown Brothers Harriman & Co. are members of the Board of Directors of the Union Pacific Corporation, and of the seven-member executive committee. Brown Brothers Harriman & Co. has no financial interest in the Union Pacific, and the stock that people think belongs to Brown Brothers Harriman is actually held by Brown Brothers Harriman for the account of their customers.

It is also important to note that the Brown Brothers partners who are identified with Union Pacific have never given a word of advice to Brown Brothers Harriman & Co., one way or the other, about what they should tell their customers about the Union Pacific. Brown Brothers Harriman has to make up its own mind about whether the Union Pacific securities are good or bad, just as any other Wall Street firm must do.

I want to repeat that we have been fortunate in the

Union Pacific in surrounding ourselves with good executives in all classifications, and good directors. It has been, I think, an outstandingly happy organization. We have worked together with little or no jealousies, all with the same goals in mind. I think this comes down from the atmosphere of professionalism that my father established, that Judge Lovett and Averell carried on, and that I and Bob Lovett do our best to maintain and extend.

Our labor relations appear to be satisfactory. Nowadays, all contracts are universal between all the railroads and the unions. We have been fortunate in recent years in our relations with our own labor union leaders. Our presidents and officers, having mostly come up through the ranks, know the conditions. Most of our employees are men of long tenure, old-timers if you like. And so I think we have had, by and large, a very happy relationship, although it is a continuous and continuing effort.

For instance, one day I met our vice-president of labor relations in Chicago as I was passing through. I said, "What are you doing here?" He said, "We've got the negotiations on which I've been spending every day for the last ten years." That is what I mean. Intelligent labor relations need constant attention and get constant attention.

Finally, we were able to create a Union Pacific Foundation. Under the state laws of Utah, in which the Union Pacific is chartered, a corporation was not allowed to give its money away except for the benefit of stockholders. We had been making donations under those specifications, some of them a little stretched, and we gave substantial amounts of money to the Red Cross long before I was an officer of the Red Cross. In all this nobody objected.

However, we thought we ought to organize our philanthropic activities more formally, and we decided to create a Union Pacific Foundation. This necessitated an attempt to make appropriate changes in the state laws. So we embarked upon a novel procedure: we made a test donation, and then we had a couple of stockholders bring suit against us to challenge the basis of the gift. In the courts, we were upheld, a constitutional basis was established and the state laws were soon changed to let the Union Pacific Foundation get under way.

It was during this lawsuit, incidentally, that I was cited as a test case myself in, of all things, the *Journal of the American Medical Association*. At this time, the *Journal* was running an editorial campaign against the gobbledy-gook doctors often use while writing their papers. The *Journal* was also against excessive legalese and it found encouragement in our Union Pacific Foundation test case. One of the lawyers asked me a question that seemed to me to ramble on and on without point. So I took it upon myself to rephrase the question: "Do you mean, do corporations give more money now than they used to?" I answered my own question with one word, "Yes." The *Journal* held me up to its readers as a shining example.

Since that day, the Union Pacific Foundation has been a successful enterprise. Under our policy, we confine our philanthropy to the states and communities the Union Pacific serves, and this has developed considerable good will in these regions. We consult our local Union Pacific people when we are considering making grants in their respective territories. In general, we take great care in weighing and measuring the many applications we receive, and we hope we are good corporate neighbors.

Each year, the Union Pacific Corporation—at first, it

was the railroad company—gives a round sum to the Foundation, which distributes the money where it is most needed and, frankly, where it will do the railroad some good. This is the way it should be, in my judgment, and deciding on the specific merits is a difficult and challenging job. In corporate as in personal philanthropy, it is quite something to be able to give money away with an intelligent awareness of priorities.

I cannot claim to have originated the Union Pacific Foundation, and in this a great deal of the credit should go to Frederick Warburg, then one of our directors. He talked at great length with me about the possibilities, and I supported him wholeheartedly. It was always a question of working the thing out properly, and now I believe we have done this.

Right now, the Foundation is proceeding along rather novel lines. It is encouraging prospective donees to come up with programs in which, with seed capital, substantial savings can be made in routine operating costs. For example, the Massachusetts Institute of Technology in Cambridge, Massachusetts, came up not long ago with an idea for a survey of its own in-plant energy consumption. MIT is not on the Union Pacific line, but it does help train our engineers and other technical personnel, so it was deemed to qualify for help from us. MIT was awarded $28,000 for a start of the survey, and its skilled people found out how they could save an astonishing $800,000 a year simply by managing their boilers, lighting and all their other routine facilities more efficiently.

The Foundation has made approximately twenty grants of a similar nature in recent years and has therefore been useful in combating rising costs and inflationary pressures.

I should point out that Union Pacific's environmental expenditures are financed entirely from our business operations. We are spending millions of dollars for ecological benefit, and I could philosophize at length about how conservationists and businessmen should be friends. There is a great deal to be said on both sides of the traditional ecology-energy argument, but we are going to have to find a middle ground, and I am convinced that we will be able to. As of now, in my opinion, the pendulum has swung too far over to the ecology side.

For example, the Union Pacific has considerable deposits of low-sulphur coal, which creates only minimal amounts of smog. One day we received an inquiry from Gary, Indiana, one of the most seriously smog-ridden towns in the country. A utility company in Gary wanted to be supplied with our low-sulphur coal. We could provide this by opening up a mine in a remote section of Wyoming and constructing a nine-mile spur of railroad track to bring the coal down to the main line for shipment to Gary.

However, we were told we would have to prepare an environmental impact statement, which would take some months, detailing exactly how our new spur would not foul the sagebrush and all the rest of it. We began to work up our statement, while Gary spent several more months in its smog. We admitted that the only thing that might conceivably foul the atmosphere in that part of the boondocks would be the emission from a single diesel moving up and down the spur.

While Gary choked on, our procedure dragged on, but we finally got permission to build our spur. If there had been no energy crisis, we might still be applying, and

Gary might still be choking, and the low-sulphur coal would be staying right there in the ground.

This leaves me with little more to say about my life in the Union Pacific, except for perhaps a footnote or two. I would point out, for example, that geography itself has been and still is a great element in the success of the Union Pacific. The railroads in trouble are the ones that operate under densely populated, short-haul conditions, in particular competition with passenger automobiles and, of course, with trucks. Not only the Union Pacific, but other western railroads and some of the southern railroads benefit from long-haul operations.

For example, we now have trains that go all the way through from Jacksonville, Florida, to the Pacific Northwest, over the lines of several railroad companies, and the makeup of the trains is not touched from point of departure to point of arrival. Even the same power goes through with nothing more than a change of train crews. This is just one example of the arrangements that are now being made between the railroads, with which the Union Pacific interchanges its freight, to the immense benefit of shippers in terms of time and costs. This is good for the country, too, because some 20 per cent of the cost of all goods reflects the cost of transportation.

This new trend reinforces the case, which I have stated for years, for an integrated national transportation policy, and we have a few hopeful signs. One is a bill in Congress designed to reduce the level of government regulation. There are still too many people pulling at cross-purposes, one in favor of the rails, another for air, another for highways and another for canals and barge lines, when what is wanted is for everybody to pull together.

The day will come, however, and I am sure of this, when a shipper will be able to go into one integrated transportation office and say, for example, "I want to ship my goods, and I am in no hurry." He will be advised how to use the most appropriate chain of services to get his goods where he wants to, and when, at the lowest cost.

Or this shipper will be able to walk in and say, "I'm in an awful hurry," or even, "I'm in an intermediate hurry," or something like that. He will be advised how best to ship his goods to meet his delivery requirements. No more will the shipper have to shop around truckers and rail yards and airlines and every place else before he can conduct his business efficiently.

So let me wind up this discussion of my years in the Union Pacific on a typical note—sounding off.

As much as anything else in my life, and sometimes a little more, the Union Pacific has been fun.

I still remember the train whistle in the first years of the century.

I still commend to my countrymen the thrill of that inscription on the monument at Promontory, Utah:

"The last rail is laid! The last spike is driven! The Pacific Railroad is completed!"

CHAPTER VIII: TRAVELS AND ADVENTURES

To E.R.H.

A sportsman—who in sports is fair and generous
—a good loser and a gracious winner.
With deep gratitude for always taking me along.

G.F.H.

When I sometimes read the dedication that Gladys
wrote to me in her book *Hits and Misses* I often think
how well I had her fooled. I think it was typical that she
was so thoughtful to link me with her fine volume of
reminiscences. But it is I who am grateful to her for coming along with me on so many wonderful and interesting
journeys. We have had a very full life together, con-
tinually together, in business and in the Red Cross, in our
home life and on our trips.

On our journeys in particular her terrific quality of enthusiasm emerged even more than usual, and she had a
fantastic time because of her capabilities, both physical
and mental. I remember one hunting trip we took to-

153

gether into the Salmon River country in Idaho. She was assigned the second guide, who was one of the few unfortunate people we ever had on our trips. The first day, this fellow took her on a hike for miles, just to wear her out. He was overheard remarking, after they got back to camp, "That will fix my dude."

Well, bright and early the next morning, Gladys was on deck. The guide was the one who was sorry he had to go out again.

She has a great zest for life. She likes people, she likes places, and she is inquisitive. Fortunately, we like the same things and the same people, and this has just made all the difference. We have had fun, a lot of fun. There have been some disagreements, of course, naturally always my fault. She was not an outdoors girl, primarily, when we married, although she had ridden a bit in Central Park in New York City, had shot quail at her father's place in the South and played good golf. She came into a family that were ardent horsemen, hunters, shooters and travelers, and she fitted in superbly, fortunately for her, and fortunately for me.

Because so many of these travels and adventures did concern hunting, I should make it clear at the start that what we loved was the game. It was not the shooting. It was the life we led, the company we had. We still have a few of our choice heads mounted on the walls of our home at Arden, and these are not trophies to gloat over, but souvenirs to remind us of the things we did together.

Once we motored with our daughters Betty and Phyllis from Paris to St. Moritz. I had heard so much about St. Moritz from Gladys that I wanted to see it. Then we drove back through Munich and some of the old World War I battlefields in northeastern France.

Once in the early 1930s, when I was on a long business trip to England, we took a house for the summer on the golf links at Sunningdale, near London, and that was a great experience, with one of the great English golf courses at our front door. We went up to Scotland for grouse shooting at somebody else's expense, and we enjoyed it. But the exciting thing was stalking stag on the moors in September. We had hunted game in several countries, but in Scotland you did it all in the open. You could see what reaction the animal had, if he saw you, or scented you. It was a great education, and I became a better hunter for the experience.

One of the moors we went to had been leased by an American friend of ours named Lloyd-Smith and his wife, who had girls about the age of our own daughters. We all went up to the moors en masse, and our daughters shot grouse and their daughters shot grouse. Their daughters stalked stag and our daughters stalked stag. It was a very fine family party.

We had another family party with the Lloyd-Smiths in Florida, when we went down together and chartered a couple of houseboats. On one of these, the Lloyd-Smiths, ourselves and the eldest daughters lived, while the younger kids lived on the second houseboat in charge of Gladys' father, Dr. Fries. After Lloyd-Smith's death, Mrs. Lloyd-Smith married none other than Knight Woolley. We did keep the whole thing in the family.

One of the years we were in England, we went over to Austria for what we hoped would be another memorable adventure. Averell had taken a lease on a place in the

Austrian Tyrol, the Schloss Wildalpen, which was a famous hunting ground for chamois and stag. We made up a party consisting of Knight Woolley, Elbridge Gerry, Neil Mallon, Margaret and Sloan Colt, and an English friend named Francis Edlmann, along with Gladys and myself. We hastened there under the spur of our instructions: "It is imperative that you arrive in Wildalpen not later than September 25 so as to be there in the roaring season." As Gladys commented: "This was a command that could not be ignored, so with due meekness, we made our plans accordingly."

Gladys continued, "We were greeted by a Dr. E. and his daughter. He was a Hungarian lawyer and acted as agent for the place.

"Just at dark, the most appalling noise was heard, sounding like feeding time in the lion's house at the zoo. The noise grew in volume, and seemed to be coming closer. 'Roaring time' in the telegram had a clear meaning. For about four or five days during the rut, the stags roared just like lions, while they came down into the valleys searching for their mates. All night long the roars continued, so loud were they it was actually difficult to get to sleep.

"At 4 A.M., a buxom Austrian maid called us and after breakfast we were each assigned to our own *Jäger*, or guide, and away we went with many a mutual shout of '*Weidmannsheil*,' the hunter's greeting.

"In fact, there were a lot of native customs in the Tyrol. When you shot an animal, your *Jäger*, who spoke no known language, would dip an evergreen, shaped in the form of a cross, into the animal's open wound. He would get some blood out of the animal and onto the evergreen.

156

Then he would stick this on his hat and hand the whole thing to you with a respectful '*Weidmannsheil!*' You took the cross, the bloody bit of evergreen, and stuck it in your own hat. You would tell the *Jäger*, '*Weidmannsdank*,' or hunter's thanks or blessing. When you arrived home that night, everybody would know how successful or un-successful you had been.

"In fact, at the end of a sojourn at Wildalpen, you were supposed to stick all your evergreens into your hat at the same time. This was a moment when the good shots looked like forests and the poor shots looked rather nude."

There is an interesting anecdote about Austria which I believe to be true even though it seems so farfetched to us. An Englishman whom I knew had once gone to one of these places in the Tyrol. He was hunting with his *Jäger* when they spotted a man on the mountainside. The *Jäger* said, "That's a poacher. Shoot him." The Englishman re-plied, "Certainly not." The *Jäger* said, "Give me your gun and I'll shoot him." Again, the Englishman refused. That evening, after they had returned to their *Schloss*, the Englishman's host said, "Your bags are being packed, and you'll take the next train." When the Englishman asked what on earth the matter was, his host said, "You refused to protect my property."

About the time I heard this story, we had a contrary ex-perience at Arden, where we have deer, and where we also have poachers. One of our groundsmen suddenly came across a poacher, who made a run for it, jumped into his automobile and drove off. Our man fired his shot-gun in the air hoping this might persuade the poacher to stop the car and surrender. The poacher kept on driving, but our man got the license number, and he called the police.

The authorities raided the poacher's house and there they found, sure enough, two or three carcasses of deer. After the usual legal proceedings, the poacher was fined. Not long afterward, however, a charge was brought against our groundsman for felonious assault because he had fired his shotgun into the air. We finally got him cleared of this charge, but we had a difficult time of it.

Not that hunting was the be-all and end-all of even these earlier trips, when we were both younger and stronger than we are today. The summer we were at Sunningdale, we went up to Scotland not only to shoot grouse and stalk stag, but also to play golf. This was highly delightful, but many of the golf courses only permitted women to play on one certain day a week.

Well, we were very anxious to play Troon, a very famous course. We arrived there right on Ladies' Day. However, it was blowing so hard and raining so torrentially that not a single one of the natives was out of doors. And this was in Scotland!

The rain at Troon was not coming down, it was flying sideways, and there was not another soul in sight. But Gladys and I played Troon, and we really did have the whole famous course to ourselves. This was an unforgettable memory.

In January and February 1938, Gladys and I embarked upon another voyage of adventure and exploration, this time to some of the wilder reaches of Mexico. Our companions on parts of this trip were Cornelius "Sonny" Whitney and his wife Glwadys, or Gee, and also Neil

Mallon. Neil was a Yale classmate of mine, a bachelor, the head of Dresser Industries, and he used to visit with us a great deal.

We started off by going to Guaymas, on the eastern shore of the Gulf of California. There we chartered a couple of Mexican fishing boats and chugged along the coast of Baja California. We saw country that nobody had been at. We saw Indian tribes that were still living in the most primitive conditions.

Then we went into the Yaqui Valley, one of the most wonderfully fertile valleys in the world, said to be second in its category only to the valley of the Nile. About thirty years before, a Yaqui Valley irrigation project had been launched by Harry Payne Whitney, John Henry Hammond, and a few other investors. Sonny Whitney had later moved into the situation and he was able to make a success of it, only be rewarded with expropriation by the Mexican government.

Some of the land had not yet been forfeited, however, and we were able to do some duck shooting on the Yaqui River delta, which was covered with rice fields. It was a famous winter resort for ducks, geese and other wild fowl.

We went out before daylight, and as we drove through the rice fields, we heard a roar of wings. It was literally a roar of wings as the night shift of the birds flew back to the water. As the day shift began to come in, we got settled for our shooting. But now we were astonished to see that the whole horizon was covered from one end to the other with flights of birds.

As a result, after firing only a few shots, we just sat there in admiration watching those hordes and hordes of birds come in to feed. This was an experience we would never forget. Gladys wrote in *Hits and Misses:*

"For three and a half hours we sat there and from all sides, as far as the eye could see, there were ducks in the air. The lines of flight were fantastic, all in different formation, and on different levels. Some of them were flying in a wedge, some in V-formation, others in a long, wavering line that stretched far across the valley. As you looked up into the sky, pattern after pattern of birds superimposed themselves upon each other.

"The large majority of the ducks were pintails, but we also saw mallards, widgeon, teal, canvasback and many more varieties. In addition to the duck, there were flocks of Canadian geese, whose honking filled the air, and also great flights of sandhill crane mingling their unmistakable whistlings with the other bird sounds. On and on they came, as the sun flooded the country with a soft, rosy light, the mountains became clearer, and there was that heavenly tropical freshness that is so delicious before the heat of the day."

One incident will illustrate conditions in Mexico at that time. A friend of ours had started a dairy in the Yaqui Valley because the one thing that was really needed there was fresh, clean milk for the school children. But the day the dairy opened for business, one of the local leaders got one of the bottles of milk, injected some poison into it with a hypodermic syringe and promptly had it analyzed. When the results were announced, the propaganda was put out that the Americans had started their dairy just to kill Mexican babies.

Next, we took the train to Guadalajara, the second city of Mexico. We were still riding on the Southern Pacific

Railroad, because the line had not yet been taken over. Guadalajara was not yet the thriving modern city it is today, and we saw a lot of old things, markets, primitive factories, and it was quite an experience.

Our own Grumman Goose picked us up in Guadalajara and took us on to Mexico City. We were fascinated by the ancient monuments, the silversmithing in the surrounding villages and especially the horsemen and -women who rode daily in the park, all bedecked with silver and gold trappings on their clothes and on their saddles.

In Mexico City, however, both Gladys and I were disgusted by the bullfight we attended. One thing that impressed us when we first went into the so-called plaza was the shoddiness of the bull ring. It was a dirty, filthy place, completely scarred with advertisements for beer and what not, and we started out with a healthy prejudice in favor of the bull.

I must say, the ritual of the bullfight was fascinating to watch, particularly in the Portuguese style, in which the matador fights the bull from horseback. But the Spanish style was just as revolting.

At one point, the bull seemed to be doing very well, and we were hoping the bull would get the matador. The matador even had to jump out of the bull ring. But the matador won—and we walked out.

Then we flew to the Yucatán to see the Mayan ruins. They were a primitive people, but they had been way ahead in many features. They did not have the wheel, but had a calendar more accurate than the one extant in Europe at that time.

The Mayan ruins at Chichén Itzá were extraordinarily fascinating. I shall not soon forget their ball court, an area about three quarters the size of a football field, boxed in on two sides by high walls. Within was a small stone ring, about the size of a basketball basket, on each side. The Mayans played their strange game with a rubber ball. They could butt the ball, or kick it, or bounce it off their shoulders, but they could not use their hands. They had to put the ball through this little bitty ring. Evidently it was a very intense game, more than anything we have in our culture, because the winners could demand all kinds of tribute from the losers.

The winners could even demand human sacrifices, and there was a mural that showed the taking of human life after one of these games. They were playing the game for life or death.

One night, we went out to the ball court, which was still in an extraordinarily good condition, and sat on a small stone pedestal at one end of the field. At the other end, approximately one hundred yards away, was another stone pedestal on which somebody placed a Victrola and began to play symphonic music. The acoustics were so perfect we could hear the music very clearly in the tropical night, right down to the remotest notes.

The Carnegie Institute people at Chichén Itzá showed us some of the ruined temples and other buildings they and their predecessors had discovered in the jungle. They showed us how the Mayans had lived, and I was increasingly impressed by their industriousness. For example, their main source of food was corn, and the only way they could grow corn was to clear the jungle, take a fertile field, use a stick to make a hole and drop a kernel into the ground. They did not rotate crops, and so, after a few years, this particular part of their land would become sterile. They would move on to another part of the jungle and repeat the process, growing corn, building temples, and they have left us many of the wonders of the world.

Gladys summed up her sentiments about this trip, which I heartily shared. She wrote: "Already, I have a strong nostalgia for Mexico. The clear blue waters, the high, jagged mountains, the flowers with their brilliant colors and delicious smells, the little burros with their beguiling faces, the natives in their serapes and rebozos, the Mayan ruins, yes, even the dust which has no equal, all has started to haunt me. I can hardly wait to return."

Along about 1930, one of my friends was Grover Loening, a fine fellow who was one of the pioneers in the design and construction of amphibious airplanes. One day, I was given a ride in one of these amphibians, from some place in Long Island to the waters of the East River at the very foot of Wall Street itself.

That was a gorgeous flight, and I arrived at the office as fresh as a daisy. I began to think, why not try commuting in an amphibian?

Near Arden there was a lake, only a couple of miles from the house, and it struck me there was ample water space on this lake to permit takeoffs and landings. And at the other end of the commuter run, there was always the East River.

So I went and bought one of the first amphibians—a Loening job. It had a top speed, as I recall, of 80 mph. One afternoon we were flying up the Hudson River on our commuter route home, and we were battling against a strong headwind. I vividly remember a New York Central freight train on the tracks below. I remember it because the lumbering train actually passed us.

The amphibian served its purpose well, and I loved it, and then I learned that a new concern, the Grumman Aircraft Corporation, was going into the business of amphibian planes. Grumman had designed and built a mock-up of a very comfortable four-seater amphibian aircraft which they named the "Goose." After a lot of discussion, four friends and I each put in orders for the new planes. These five were the first orders Grumman received, and we put the company on the map. Since then, their Navy fighters helped us win the Pacific war, and their famous moon module has taken our astronauts sight-seeing on the moon.

That Grumman Goose served me well on many long-distance trips. In August and September 1938, Gladys and I, accompanied by Betty and Phyllis, flew to British Columbia. Once again, we were headed for one of the wildest sections of the continent and once again, we relied heavily upon our own Grumman Goose, in which we flew to Edmonton, Alberta, taking two days to get there.

After a two-day layover at Edmonton because of foul weather, we picked up our Canadian pilot, a World War I fighter ace named Wop May, who was to guide us into the wilderness. He had thirteen German planes to his credit and he had been one of the aviators sent up to serve as bait for the Red Baron, Manfred von Richthofen, the day the German was brought down.

The two idle days were put to good use because we were to fly where there were no maps at all for the route, so there was a lot of planning to do. Also we had friends in Edmonton, Americans by name of the Curt Munsons, with whom it was a joy to spend the time.

Anyway, when we finally got off, we flew into a cheerfully named lake, Deadman's Lake, where we rendezvoused with our outfit, which had spent three weeks packing in.

Once there, we had a magnificent time of it, with the family all together. The country was rugged and beautiful, and the mosquitoes were rugged. The animals and the flora were new to us. We were able to secure a good sheep's head and there were a couple of billy goats who were rather respectable in size.

On one of the best days when we all got our sheep, Gladys and I went to one end of a valley and the girls went to the other end. The scenery was beautiful and we loved everything about it. Gladys and her guide, I with my guide, and the girls with their one guide between them all went off in different directions. But one really frustrating part of sheep and goat hunting was that we had to climb a mountain just so we could look around. Invariably, we would spot a billy goat or sheep on the mountain opposite to the one we were on. So we would have to climb down and climb up the other side. By this time, our prey would have wandered off somewhere else.

But this was all part of the game, and this was what we loved. We stayed in the wilds about three weeks and then returned to our ranch in Idaho. We planned to return to British Columbia the following year, with the same outfit. This time, however, we planned to leave our guns behind and go hunting with our cameras. But World War II began in Europe in September 1939 and we decided to stay home.

Before the onset of World War II, in February and March 1939, Gladys and I flew down in the Goose to Guatemala. This was and still is a beautiful country. It rises from sea level, which is tropical backwash, steaming hot and humid, all the way up to very high mountains. Guatemala City, the capital, is up around five thousand feet in a wonderful climate. There we were the guests of the president of the railroad that ran from coast to coast and served the banana industry.

One of the first Guatemalans we met on this trip was the President of Guatemala, Jorge Ubico. He had been President for eight years before we got there, and he seemed to have everything very much under control. He was a despot, a benevolent despot, and he was going great guns with the country. He was building roads and schools and the people seemed to be happy and satisfied.

It was strange one day when we were out sight-seeing, when a motorcyclist roared up beside us. We saw it was a uniformed official and we wondered what we had done. But it was the bearer of an official invitation to attend a reception at the presidential palace.

The presidential reception was quite a sight, quite a sight. It was a lot of fun to see what happened after we had all passed through the receiving line. The men went one way, into one section of the palace, and all the women went the other way, Gladys among them. I remember that when we left I shook hands with President Ubico and offered to trade him for our President.

Mr. Armstrong, our host, and his wife, a Guatemalan, took us everywhere. We saw the highways and byways of Guatemala. Each town had its market day, and we arranged our trips so that we would get to the different villages on these days. The markets were a riot of color, as all the surrounding natives brought in their goods, usually on their backs and on their heads. The people were mostly of Indian stock, but they were all Catholics, a natural result of the Spanish invasion in the 1500s. We had to hand it to the Catholic Church. They did a great job of helping to organize civilization in Guatemala.

One thing that went wrong, however, was that the Guatemalans appeared to think our cameras were evil eyes. They would not let us take their pictures. I had heard some rumors about this before we went down, and I had bought a weird gadget, a right-angled viewfinder. With this I was able to appear to be looking at right angles away from those whose picture I was about to take.

Another thing that went wrong was that I came down with a cold, and later with dysentery, which took a long time to get over. At that time, there was no cure for this complaint and it left me weak and debilitated for months to come. This was my own stupidity. I had been very careful everywhere I traveled, even to the point of boiling the toothbrush water. But there was a very fine little inn, tiny but very nice, run by some English people. For dessert they had strawberries, and like a damned fool, I ate the strawberries!

But the Guatemalans were such wonderful people—they had so much grace and style—that when they came to visit me, they expressed their sorrow that this had happened to me in Guatemala.

Finally, it was out to the airport and a sad farewell. About our hosts, the Armstrongs, Gladys commented, "No two guests could ever have been more trouble, and no two hosts could have been kinder; anticipating each thought and wish, they did everything for our comfort and pleasure, no matter how much trouble to themselves it entailed."

Alas, this was to be the last time Gladys and I were to take one of these journeys. I have not left the United States, in fact, since then. During the war, Averell was away so often on government service that I more or less stayed home looking after the store. After the war it seemed more appropriate for the younger partners of Brown Brothers Harriman to make the necessary journeys overseas and re-establish the necessary contacts. I was also so busy with my increasing responsibilities with the American Red Cross that I could not get away.

When World War II began, private flying was taboo, and so I parted with my Goose and sold it for a nominal sum to the Royal Canadian Air Force. The reason I mention this is that in 1941, at the meeting between Roosevelt and Churchill off the coast of Newfoundland at which the Atlantic Charter was signed, what should turn up but my old Grumman to pick up my brother, Averell, who was in the American party.

After the war, I bought a Grumman Widgin, which was a smaller edition of the Goose, with a limited speed and range. I used it only for commuting and for short hops such as to Washington. In fact, this aircraft remained in service until only a year or so ago, it was so well maintained. But the pilot I had had since the 1930s, Cliff Kernochan, had become sixty-five, and I was older than that. Also, the smog in New York City had developed to the point that we were often unable to fly. So, in a nutshell, the pilot, myself and our aircraft reached a ripe old age simultaneously.

Incidentally, I actually got more for the Widgin when I sold it than what I had paid for it twenty-five years before. That speaks well for the quality of Grumman products. It also speaks for our maintenance and for the rate of inflation. While none are built these days, amphibians are in great demand, especially in places like Alaska, where they are extremely useful.

But there always was our ranch in Idaho. My father had bought a half interest in it, sight unseen, in 1908, on the recommendation of Judge Lovett. The latter, with his son, Bob, had visited the ranch at the invitation of one of the Guggenheim brothers of copper fame, who were the owners at the time.

The Island Park Land and Cattle Company, the ranch's official name, had been started by four officials of the Oregon Short Line in the early 1890s by buying out the holdings of a number of early settlers or homesteaders. Because of their occupation, the ranch was nicknamed "Railroad Ranch," as it has been known to the present day.

While the Short Line men used it for recreation, hunting and fishing, the ranch has always been in the cattle business as its main function, as it is today. Because of the abundance of lush nutritious grasses, cattle fatten quickly in the summer months. But the long, hard winters, with snowfalls of up to nine feet, are a different matter. In later years this difficulty has been met by moving the cattle to the lower valley during winter periods for feeding purposes. About one half of the ranch's capacity for young stock is raised from its own cows, with the balance being bought as calves. At the proper age and weight, the grass-fed steers and heifers are sold to feeders for final fattening before they are sent to the slaughterhouse.

Anyway, my father never got to the ranch and it was 1912 before my mother took Averell, my sister Carol and myself, together with a number of our young friends, for our first visit.

It was a matter of love at first sight for all of us. The glorious scenery and weather, the fishing, the hunting, the horseback riding and learning the lore of cattle handling all combined to lure us back there summer after summer. My mother continued her visits until shortly before her death in 1932. Averell, together with his wife, continued for some years, but Gladys and I have only missed war years for our annual treks, counting up now to about sixty of such visits. In fact, I have had a running argument with the last two governors of Idaho, telling them that I question the reasoning that requires me, after all those years, to buy a non-resident fishing license just because I have not lived in Idaho the necessary six consecutive months to qualify for a resident license. On the other hand, I have several times spent the necessary six weeks to qualify for divorce proceedings—never, of course, utilized. I said I thought something was screwy. In rebuttal the governors stated that in Idaho first things come first.

In 1954, together with Charles S. Jones, president of Richfield Oil, I bought out the Guggenheim heirs. This move resulted in a long and friendly partnership with Charlie and his delightful wife, Jenny. In 1961 Charlie decided to withdraw as a partner and I bought him out, but the Jones family remained as welcome tenants, as

Jenny still does since Charlie's death. Since then Averell and I have been sole proprietors.

Throughout the years, in typical Harriman fashion, we have invited many friends to accompany us and when our daughters were growing up included other youngsters to enjoy the unique life we lead.

At the outset we were almost completely isolated with only a few neighbors at several miles' distance. Now, of course, civilization has moved in. But the country is vast, the air and the water remain unpolluted and the late summer and early fall climate is ideal.

Situated as we are with four miles of the north fork of the Snake River flowing through our lands, we are fortunate in fabulous trout fishing. In fact, our friends tell us we have the best dry-fly fishing on this continent, and many are in a position to know what they are talking about.

Then too, for many years we indulged in the fascinating and unique sport of bear hunting with hounds which we followed on horseback. Because of the mountainous countryside, heavily timbered, we could not keep the hounds in sight, but tried to follow on ridge tops within sound of the hounds' voices. In most cases the bear eventually went up a tree, but only if we had some dude along who had never shot a bear did we make a kill.

Originally the birds—ducks, geese and many species of grouse—were plentiful, but the big game such as deer, elk and moose had already been nearly exterminated by the trappers and early settlers, who regarded all food animals as "fair game." That there are now more elk is due to a fortuitous set of circumstances. We had a neighbor, an early homesteader, who in a heavy early snowfall found

171

three elk cows and a bull trapped by the snow on his property. He fed them and built a fence around them. By 1915, when we bought his place, there were about fifty or sixty elk, all progeny of the original animals, even though he had shot some for food and allowed some of his friends to do likewise. We moved this herd to the home ranch, where we released them into a specially fenced pasture, killing a few from time to time for meat. By 1932 the herd, still from the original stock, numbered about a hundred and fifty, all healthy despite the strict inbreeding, a puzzle to the theorists and an attraction to sightseers. As the elk ate nearly as much hay in the winter as a steer and this was the depth of the Depression, their maintenance became quite a burden. So we made a deal with the State Game Department that we would release our elk into the neighboring government forest lands provided a permanent closed elk hunting season would be established.

Unfortunately, however, this agreement was not put in writing. Soon after World War II, when the elk population became abundant with resulting excellent hunting in non-restricted adjoining lands, the native Idaho so-called sportsmen looked with envious eyes upon the animals in the preserve. Such pressure was brought to bear that the Game Department was forced to open up hunting by permit in the preserve. This was perpetrated to such an extent that by 1970 the elk were once again virtually exterminated. This was a frustrating experience.

At the ranch we were located about equidistant from the famous Jackson Hole hunting country of Wyoming and the little-known primitive area surrounding the Salmon River and its forks in Idaho. Both afforded ideal camping country in rugged terrain with exciting opportunities to find good chances for elk and moose in the former and Rocky Mountain sheep and goats in the latter, provided we were ready and willing to really rough it and wear out our legs climbing in precipitous mountain country. This we did with relish on a number of occasions, accompanied by our daughters as they grew up.

But what we all really enjoyed in the ranch life was to help in handling the cattle. We were usually at the ranch about the time the cattle were rounded up from their summer grazing ranges and eventually driven to the railhead for shipment. As in every industry, there is a right and a wrong way to run the business. The average eastern dude's idea is to "cowboy" them at top speed. All that does is run off precious pounds of weight. The right way is to keep them moving at a slow rate and to try to outthink the steers' intentions, always prepared to act fast to head them off. This method preserves the cowboys' control of the herd and means more poundage on the scales.

By the late 1960s I thought I was pretty well steeped in the early history of our part of Idaho when the state historian paid us a visit. He asked if we had ever had an archaeological survey made. I replied, "No, but we have found quite a mass of Indian artifacts such as arrow- and spearheads, and a war club." He said, "I don't mean that modern stuff. Let me send up a team of experts from the state university." This he did and within twenty minutes of their arrival they discovered in one of our numerous stream beds the evidence of human occupation dating back eight to twelve thousand years—obsidian arrowheads and skin scrapers and such. The following summer the archaeological team made a more extended survey, confirming in detail that our part of Idaho, particularly the lands our ranch occupied, was indeed the stamping ground for prehistoric tribes. It was all very exciting.

Because we all felt such lasting gratitude for our many years of a full life at Railroad Ranch and because we just could not face the prospect of its becoming nothing more than an uncontrolled real estate development with hot dog stands and cheap honky-tonks, and because we could foresee the necessity for preserving such property for the enjoyment of future generations, Averell and I decided to give the ranch to the State of Idaho as a state park.

So we made a contract in 1961 with Governor Robert Smylie which was later confirmed by the Idaho legislature to bequeath our interests to the state in what was to be known as the Harriman State Park of Idaho. We set certain conditions, among them being that the state would undertake to enlarge our ten thousand acres of fee land with acreage from the United States government lands surrounding us, by purchase, lease or otherwise. Negotiations toward this end have already been started by the present governor, Cecil D. Andrus.

Another condition requires the state to create a game preserve of some ten thousand additional acres, forbidding hunting of any kind within its limits. This we felt was necessary not only to protect the birds and the animals, but also the lives of park visitors from trigger-happy hunters. Of course, we arranged to permit authorized state employees to control the size of animal herds in keeping with the forage available.

174

Lastly, no fish may be taken with any lure other than a feathered fly, wet or dry.

And so I think we have made proper disposition of our beloved ranch.

Nothing could rival our enjoyment of that traditional American experience, the cattle drive. Gladys described one in *Hits and Misses* unforgettably:

> *"We trailed 'em here*
> *We trailed 'em there*
> *We trailed 'em almost everywhere*
> *They filled our hearts with black despair*
> *Those 'trailing' little steers.*

"'We must leave as soon as it is light in order to make camp before dusk.' That sounded very logical. We were completing our plans for a trek of eight hundred head of cattle from Idaho to Montana, where we had acquired a winter range.

"'The boys are going to have the steers bunched up in the north corner near the gate to-night so that we won't waste any time getting under way in the morning,' said Dan, our ranch manager. It sounded better and better, just too easy for words. Our plan was to trail the beasties from our ranch to Dubois, about fifty miles away, load them there, and ship them overnight to Apex, a siding on the Union Pacific not far from Dillon, then drive them the remaining miles to their winter quarters.

"We were to make fourteen miles the first day,

and had rented a pasture enclosed by a good wire fence where we could hold them the first night. The second night we expected to reach Dubois and corral them, loading early the next morning. The plans were fine except for one thing: we neglected to explain them to the steers, and they had ideas of their own, eight hundred of them.

"Sleeping bags and duffel were loaded into the chuck wagon in the evening. In fact, everything possible was done to ensure against delay on the morrow.

"It was cold at 5 A.M. the next day—but beautiful. The stars crackled. The geese were honking fussily, and the coyotes serenading. We had twelve miles to motor to where the cattle were pastured. Here we would collect the horses, both the ones we were to ride and five mares who were in foal, who were bound for the Montana ranch.

"Dawn was just breaking as we neared the cattle ranch and, as it grew lighter, I peered out the car window, then I looked again. Not a steer in sight. In spite of the chilly air, I leaned way out of the car—yes, those little spots in the distance were the steers. They were feeding happily on the green bottomland as far from the north gate as possible. What did they care for an early start.

"Saddling quickly, we scattered in different directions to round them up. I found a good-sized bunch playing hide-and-seek in the willows and, after considerable difficulty, got them started toward the north gate. We were proceeding peacefully when we passed a bar of salt lying about fifty feet to our left and before I could wink, my little bunch was milling around the salt, smacking their long tongues in anticipation of a good lick.

"I rode over, I pushed, I whistled, I prodded and I'm positive I swore, finally I persuaded them to resume their journey—all but one—a little fuzzy fellow with a brown patch over one eye. He would start off with the crowd but the moment I rode to the other side of the bunch, back he would sneak, taking five or six would-be lickers with him. He repeated this act at least half a dozen times. I was becoming quite disgruntled when that same dogie caught a glimpse of another bunch of steers that were headed toward the gate. Forgetting the salt, he broke into a dead run—this time in the right direction— and as usual all the rest of my bunch followed.

"By the time we had counted out eight hundred head of steers and headed them on their way, it was 9:30 A.M. We had lost two and a half hours of daylight.

"Once the herd decided to move, they poured out of the gate and attacked the sagebrush at a high run, and they continued to run for a mile before we could stop them. There were seven of us riding and we had five horses to lead. As nothing is more irritating than having a horse pull back on his hackamore at the very moment you want to head off a steer, no one was over-anxious to be a 'leader.'

"Finally, we turned the herd and got them strung out on a strip of mud that goes by the name of a highway in that part of Idaho. According to schedule, we were to meet the chuck wagon that had preceded us at about noon, and have a snack. About noon, the steers were more than ready to stop and graze, but owing to our late departure we were miles from the chuck wagon.

"By this time, it was much warmer. The sun was brilliant, and the snow sparkled on the distant hills. We were all thirsty, steers, horses and men; but sagebrush, desert and water don't keep company very often. The later the hour, the slower walked the steers. They investigated minute tufts of grass. They smelled flowers. They deliberately dawdled. They couldn't see the trail. By 3:30 P.M. we were discouraged. Then, at 3:35 P.M., the front steers started to run, the next ones ran, those in the rear galloped in order to catch up. They all ran past the chuck wagon, and on and on.

"Instead of making night camp before dark, the last hour of the drive was in a blackout, as the moon had not yet risen. At long last, we reached the rented pasture and after much gentle pressure urged the cattle into it, and bedded them and ourselves down for the night. So ended the first day.

"It seemed as if we had barely gotten to sleep

before it was time to get up. I'm positive the stars hadn't budged, so short was the time. It was awfully cold and pitch black, but so beautiful. The horses were grained, saddled and tethered, the light was just breaking, and we were about to enjoy a hearty breakfast of sourdough hot cakes when a couple of restless steers pushed over the fence and found us.

"Two wouldn't have been so bad, but we knew that the other 798 would feel left out of it if they didn't come along. Two of the boys grabbed their horses and rode over to head off the bunch. The rest of us grabbed our plates and gulped down breakfast. Dan rushed about afoot doing both. With a plate in one hand, he firmly waved a fork at the invading animals.

"In a few moments we were on the march. Two of us worked to the head of the line, and tried to hold up the leaders. It was about as successful as holding water in a sieve, and by the time we were strung out, the line covered over two miles.

"On and on we plodded—sagebrush for miles in every direction, lava rock buttes, blue sky, snowy mountains, jack rabbits, eagles, air thin as gossamer, a long line of steers in front of you, their sleek backs and white faces shining, their soft, inquisitive eyes looking at you with nothing but innocence, a grand pony under you, one who loves every moment of it as much as you do and takes most of your responsibility. Is there anything more fun, or more inspiring in the world than such a day?

"After a couple of hours, the dogies became bored with the trail, and they began to straggle. First one would stray to the side, and next every steer behind him would do likewise. When you galloped up to head them back into the trail, the leader would turn and promptly rush across the trail crossways, picking up more companions as he went. Looking back, you'd see that quite a number of steers had stopped and were grazing rapidly in all directions. There was nothing for it but to lope back and frantically round them up. Just as this was accomplished, a hasty glance showed you that the ones in the lead had started up in every direction all over again. At moments, as one looked ahead or behind, you would see three of four riders frantically working their part of the line as it bulged.

"Steers love toadstools, and will rush from one to another as if possessed. We trailed over large areas of burnt ground that was covered with small tufts of fresh green grass and mushrooms. It must have tasted like caviar and pâté to the steers the way they gobbled and ran, and gobbled and ran.

"We had planned to meet the chuck wagon at midday by a creek, the only water until we reached Dubois, but because the steers trailed so badly, it was 2 P.M. before we got there. Those animals must have smelled the water a mile away, for they broke into a run, and never stopped until they got into that creek, which they swam, and continued running on the other side.

"By this time, it was far too late to tackle the remaining fifteen miles to Dubois. We did not dare attempt corralling livestock after dark as, if they ever broke on us, they would have scattered to the wind. There was nothing else to do but to remain where we were, and night-herd. We pitched camp by the creek, and on the edge of a small, flat piece of grassy ground about three acres in size. Here was good feed, and a perfect place for the cattle to bed down, and here we could water them again in the morning before starting for Dubois.

"Leaving two cowboys to round up the steers that by now were fairly scattered, we prepared camp looking forward to a good night's rest. Just at sunset, and such a sunset of flaming red, the animals were driven into their bed ground. A couple of the men stayed with them to see that they settled down while the rest of us ate some supper, and gloried in the beauty of the night. As soon as we had finished eating, Bunny and I caught up our ponies and rode slowly out to relieve the cowboys so that they might have their supper.

"It was marvelous: inky black, cold, enormous stars and fragrant sagebrush filling the air. We experience few such moments of quiet, I thought, as I rode in a slow circle round and round the bunched herd. Some of the steers

were lying down, others looked sleepy, our
horses nickered as we passed one another, riding
silently in the blackness. I hoped my "relief"
rider would not come too soon.

"All of a sudden hell popped. Steers began to
run in all directions. Those that had been lying
down jumped up. I heard Bunny shout, 'Come
over here and help me head off these cows.'
'Can't,' I screamed back. 'I'm having troubles of
my own.' The rest of the men jumped on their
ponies and came out. We all galloped up and
down and round and round. The very second
you left a spot, the steers would rush out into the
night and eternity.

"There was no peace, just plain hard riding. It
grew colder and colder. The moon came up and
dispelled some of the blackness but it also
seemed to jazz up the antics of those dogies.
Hour after hour they milled about. Later in the
night, Bunny and I tried to take a few hours off,
but sleep was out of the question. Four o'clock
saw us in the saddle, sodden, with clothes to
fight the cold. I was suffering from chilblains
and was riding in moccasins instead of boots.
My feet have never been so icy.

"At the first suspicion of light, there was no
holding the beasts any longer. They would not
even pause to drink, but tore down the trail to
Dubois. Another seven hours of trailing, trailing
here, and trailing there. For a time, they would
plod along to perfection. I'd relax, slump on my
pony, finally light a cigarette. That seemed to be

the signal for mischief, for a quarter of a mile ahead I would see the line bulge. Up I would gallop. No sooner had I left than those behind me would spread. It was the same old story. Up and down the line I'd ride on my weary pony.

"At 2 P.M., we closed the gates of the loading corral on the last steer and our sighs of relief almost created a hurricane. We couldn't start loading until 4 P.M., as a huge shipment of sheep had just been completed, and there was no room for our cars on the siding. However, by 6 P.M., the last car was loaded with our eight hundred steers and twelve horses.

"We drove into Dubois, and stopped at the pool hall to buy a newspaper. When Bunny went in, there were several men loafing about the store. One of them looked up and said, 'Well, did you get your sheep all loaded?' That was the last straw. Here we had been running after those crazy little steers for two days and nights, delivered them safely, and then, we were taken for a sheep outfit.

"We motored to the Dillon ranch in Montana, reaching there at 8 P.M., and how we enjoyed that hot lamb stew that was waiting for us, and how we enjoyed our beds that night.

"We met the train at 7 A.M. at Apex. First we led out the horses and saddled up seven for our use. The others ran loose. Then out came the steers. Dan instructed some of us to keep the first ones out bunched up until all were off the train. Well, when those steers came off the train, they started walking and they kept right on walking. Nothing could stop them. But fortunately, they decided to walk in the right direction. The loose horses added to the general gaiety but finally, at 11 A.M., we closed the Montana ranch gate after the last steer and horse had passed through it.They were safe on their winter range.

"As soon as they got inside the fence, they all decided that they wanted to lie down, which they promptly did, gazing up at us with the sweetest, most confidential expression of pleasure. It was literally the first time that they had really been still since leaving Idaho. Of course, now it didn't matter, as they were behind a good fence.

"I hated to say goodbye to those dogies, in spite of their whimsies. But I treasure a lovely picture in my mind of a sapphire sky, snow-capped mountains, pastures of good feed bordered with colorful willow bushes, flaming aspen, and—eight hundred fat, saucy steers quietly resting."

CHAPTER IX: THE GOOD NEIGHBOR I

Not long after I became president of the American National Red Cross, in the fall of 1950, I was interviewed by commentator Charles Collingwood on CBS. He outlined to me in advance the questions he was going to ask me and all went well, and we finished the scheduled cross-examination about two or three minutes before time ran out. So he popped an impromptu question at me. He asked, "What does the Red Cross need most right now?"

My immediate response was, "To be understood."

After the program was over, he said, "My God, I thought you were going to say money." But the fact of the matter is that the Red Cross did, and still does, need understanding more even than money. That is the one major difficulty the Red Cross has always had. Everybody knows what the Cancer Fund is, and what the Heart Fund does, but the Red Cross is often thought to be little more than a sprawling bureaucracy.

I believe that the American National Red Cross is one of the finest things in the whole world, and I am sure that it is an American institution in which all our people can take intense pride. But what is it? Let me therefore commence this story of my years with the Red Cross by quoting here the official statement of "The Mission of the American Red Cross." It reads:

"The American Red Cross is the instrument chosen by the Congress to help carry out the obligations assumed by the United States under certain international treaties known as the Geneva, or Red Cross Conventions. Specifically, its Congressional charter imposes on the American Red Cross the duties to act as the medium of voluntary relief and communication between the American people and their armed forces, and to carry on a system of national and international relief to prevent and mitigate suffering caused by disasters.

"All the activities of the American Red Cross and its chapters support these duties.

"Nationally and locally, the American Red Cross is governed by volunteers, most of its duties are performed by volunteers, and it is financed by voluntary contributions."

The American Red Cross dates back, in a sense, to the Battle of Solferino in Italy in 1859. A young Swiss businessman named Henri Dunant was traveling in that part of Italy in which the French had defeated the Austrians in one of the struggles for Italian unity and independence. The traveler was horrified to find the battlefield and the surrounding countryside littered with the wounded and the dying of both armies, who were receiving little or no attention. He rallied some of the local citizens and did what he could to help alleviate the agony.

When he got home to Switzerland, he wrote an article about the aftermath of Solferino and sent it to the heads of several European countries, recommending that an organization be formed to reduce suffering in wars. Perhaps to his surprise, they all reacted very favorably, and in August 1864, eleven nations signed the First Treaty of Geneva. This was the birth of the Red Cross.

The United States did not take part in this movement for fear of jeopardizing its traditional isolationism, but it did send observers to Red Cross meetings. Clara Barton, the renowned American nurse during the Civil War, was intensely interested in the Red Cross concept. She committed her prestige to the Red Cross movement, and in 1881 she succeeded in forming the American Association of the Red Cross. She thought this was a humanitarian undertaking that was certainly not a foreign entanglement.

The American Red Cross went to work in the peaceful years of the late nineteenth century to help the victims of natural disasters. This activity became known as the American Amendment to the Geneva Convention. The Red Cross, in those days, really was Clara Barton, and she enlisted the help of volunteers, doctors, nurses and other skilled people to save lives and relieve suffering in a series of devastating forest fires in Michigan and in the wake of the famous Johnstown flood in Pennsylvania.

Clara Barton was joined by another very dynamic woman, Mabel Boardman, but unfortunately they did not get along. Eventually, Miss Barton retired at the age of eighty-two in 1904 after persuading the United States Congress to incorporate the American Red Cross in 1900. Miss Boardman carried on.

In 1906, the Red Cross was subjected to its most severe test after the San Francisco earthquake—and it was then that my own family began their involvement with the Red Cross, which has lasted to this day.

When my father got the news of the disaster, he was in New York, and he immediately ordered his special train to get him to California as rapidly as possible. On that journey, he broke the east to west transcontinental railroad speed record. He parked his business car on the Oakland pier, surveyed the smoldering ruins and set out to do what he could.

In the meantime, he had already ordered the railroad to take the refugees out of town free of charge. He said that anybody who wanted to leave San Francisco need only go down to the depot and get on the train.

On the scene, my father now ordered that all relief goods should be freighted in by the railroad free of charge, and as he prowled around the devastated city, he became something of a popular hero. He was really helping to re-establish a stricken community, and he was serving almost as a one-man Red Cross.

Well, the real Red Cross consisted at that time of Miss Boardman, two men who were considered to be disaster experts, and a secretary. When President Theodore Roosevelt made a proclamation that the Red Cross would be the official relief agency in San Francisco, the two disaster experts sped out there. They were met by a hostile committee of San Francisco leaders, who told them, "Get the hell out of here. Go on home. We know what we need."

Well, my father called in the two Red Cross officials and some of the civic leaders to see him. In fact, he called them on the carpet. He said, "Stop arguing about all this nonsense. You in the town know what you need. You in the Red Cross know how to get it, and how to operate it.

Why don't you get together and work together instead of fighting one another?" Such was my father's power and presence, they did.

One of the problems now was that the wheat millers of the Middle West kept sending relief in the form of raw flour. Unfortunately, every baking oven in San Francisco had been destroyed so the flour just rotted where it lay. But my father intervened once again, and he put an embargo on all railroad shipments of flour. He allotted the train space to more urgently needed supplies.

So my father performed yeoman service in the San Francisco disaster and, what is more important, so did the Red Cross. The disaster experts and the civic leaders worked handsomely and generously together, and set a style for community cooperation in disasters that has lasted ever since.

My mother was also extremely interested in the Red Cross during its very early days. She was responsible for furnishing one of the Union Pacific's railroad cars as a traveling Red Cross first-aid instruction headquarters. The car used to visit isolated communities, where people were taught the rudiments of first aid and thus could help prevent suffering from personal disaster.

During World War I, my mother became a member of what they called the War Council of the Red Cross, and she maintained her interest in the organization until her death.

In the meantime, my wife had become involved in the Red Cross, dating from approximately 1920, when she had become a volunteer in our local chapter near Arden. In the years between the wars, she maintained her activity in Red Cross matters. She used to come home and

regale me and our daughters with stories about everything she had been doing during the day. I always teased
her. I said our daughters would marry and get out of our
house just so they would not have to listen to all the
stories about the Red Cross. But we were all Red Cross
enthusiasts.

In fact, as far as my wife was concerned, I obeyed the
old injunction that "If you can't lick 'em, join 'em." This
was an opportune moment, because it was now 1942, and
the United States was in World War II. I was too old for
military service, and I was anxious to do something constructive for the war effort. I was asked to become chairman of the Metropolitan Camp and Hospital Council of
the Greater New York area of the Red Cross, and I accepted the position with pride.

One of the main functions of the Red Cross is to be the
liaison between the armed forces and the public—this is
written in the statement of the Red Cross mission—and
there was never a time when this was more needed than
in World War II. We had our volunteers busy in military
camps and hospitals, and also on the Army piers. One of
these volunteers was Gladys, who supervised much of our
best work on these piers. In her diary, she wrote about
some Army recruits:

"Somehow, they did not look too fit, and perhaps they
had not been in training too long. Some of the boys could
hardly stand up under the heavy load they were carrying
and several were white with the strain and looked pa-
thetically nervous. As the line came to a halt, the Red
Cross canteen women stepped out and dispensed coffee
and doughnuts, chocolate and cigarettes. These boys
were grim and brought a lump into my throat."

She had a different view of some experienced combat soldiers, homeward bound, passing through: "An Army band was playing hot jitterbug tunes, and the boys that landed were brown and sunburned, husky and fit, and they carried their equipment as though it weighed a mere nothing, tossing their duffel bags to the dock as if they were mere handkerchiefs. As we took the coffee and doughnuts along the lines, the boys were friendly and joked with us. I do not know which group made my heart ache more."

Gladys finally came upon a third detachment: "They were Army nurses, a fine-looking lot, trim, well set-up and marching along under full equipment like the men. For every four or five of the nursing officers, there came an Army man, there to readjust the loads of equipment if they slipped, or were too much for the nurses. The men were never needed, as far as I could tell."

In 1944, the manager of the North Atlantic area of the Red Cross was transferred to take charge of the Pacific War area. I was asked, although still a volunteer, whether I would like to take his place as North Atlantic manager. I did not hesitate, and for the rest of the war I served as manager with jurisdiction over 411 chapters of the Red Cross in nine northeastern states. In the following year, Gladys, who during the war had been a volunteer in the area, became Chairman for Volunteers for the New York Chapter of the Red Cross. It seemed that in war, as in peace, we were destined to do almost everything together.

At the peak of World War II, the American Red Cross had approximately 3,500 chapters serving every county in the United States. This was a massive effort, and nothing like it had ever been seen in the world before. Wherever a chapter was formed, it was by petition from a qualified group in the community for a charter from the national organization. Then, as now, there was a general policy of the Red Cross, as enacted by the national Board of Governors, but the Board of Directors of the local chapters also had a certain autonomy to conduct themselves and their services in conformity with the needs and requirements of their communities.

The Red Cross had been designated by the government to be active with the troops up to and including the front lines, and our field directors were right up there with the advanced units of our armies as we moved northward through Italy and, finally, made the D-day landings in France. Many of them became war casualties.

The American Red Cross also did wonders, in my opinion, in setting up hotels, clubs and snack bars in cities behind the lines. There were also Clubmobiles, a brilliant idea, in which trailers staffed by professional and volunteer Red Cross girls would bring coffee, doughnuts and conversation from home literally up to the areas at the front.

Unfortunately, the Red Cross ran into criticism for some of its wartime operations, and much of this criticism was unfair. There were a great many American Red Cross men and women volunteers on all fronts, and they had been given the nominal rank of officers by the War Department. The rationale was that, in the event of capture, they would be treated as officers. But the War Department also had rules that women officers were allowed to go out only with men officers or civilians, and specifically not with enlisted men. Naturally, enlisted men asked Red Cross girls for dates, and when they were turned down, they blamed the Red Cross.

Many of the Red Cross operations in the war zone expanded so rapidly there was inevitable bungling. The Red Cross prepared millions and millions of packs of popular brands of cigarettes, with the imprint "Gift of the Red Cross." Well, these Red Cross cigarettes were shipped over by the armed forces with a lot of other PX material. The PX operators were not too particular which cigarettes they put on their shelves and so, to the horror of our volunteers, Red Cross cigarettes stamped "Gift of the Red Cross" would be sold to the enlisted men.

When the enlisted men left one of these PXs, they might have run into friends, who congratulated them on their good fortune in obtaining these gift Red Cross cigarettes. They would reply, "The hell we did, we had to pay for them." In no time, a rumor spread through the theater of operations that the Red Cross was selling the cigarettes it had been given for free by the folks back home.

Of course, many of the enlisted men were not smoking the cigarettes they obtained free and they were selling them on the black market, or using them for other celebrated purposes. It was also true that some enlisted men stationed in cold climates would receive heavy sweaters, for example, knitted by our volunteers at home, and when these men were shifted to warmer fronts, they would sell them. Well, every sweater, every garment so knitted was marked "Gift of the Red Cross." It was only a matter of time before another rumor went around that the Red Cross was selling gift clothing.

Sometimes I thought that the Red Cross was just going

through the same spate of criticism and unpopularity in World War II that the YMCA had gone through in World War I. The YMCA also got hell for all the fine work it did. But this did upset me terribly, and it made me damned mad, because I knew it was all a bunch of lies, and there was not much we could do about it. It was interesting that several of our volunteers, when they returned from Europe, undertook to travel across the country on their own time, and at their own expense, to tell the story about the Red Cross war effort in Europe and in the Pacific. They told the people all the rumors were damned lies, and they were very effective spokeswomen for the cause for which they had sacrificed so much.

Now that many years have passed, I would venture to suggest that the American Red Cross Clubs, the Club-mobiles, the volunteers, the field directors are among the happier memories of an unhappy time in our history. I am sure this is so for most of the young men and women who, though the time was unhappy, were indeed devoting themselves to the defense of freedom.

Incidentally, the support mission was maintained through the Korean and Vietnam conflicts, and not long ago, I received spectacular proof that we were still doing our duty. A young fellow stationed in West Germany rushed into our field director's office. He said, "I've just been speaking to my wife on the telephone, and she tells me she has swallowed an overdose of sleeping pills to commit suicide."

The field director promptly got in touch with the twenty-four-hour emergency service maintained at American Red Cross national headquarters in Washington. We have full use of the military's worldwide communications network. The national headquarters contacted the local chapter nearest the wife's home in Colorado. The local chapter called the police, who arranged for an ambulance to be sent to the home which rushed the wife to the hospital. She was pumped out just in time. The hospital told the chapter, the chapter told national headquarters and national headquarters told the field director. The serviceman was still sitting in his office when the field director told him, "It's going to be all right." The whole thing had taken just fifty-two minutes.

I should point out at this time, and I probably should have before, that the International Red Cross was and is a separate organization. This is made up entirely of Swiss citizens, and they are appointed by the Geneva Convention to be the representatives of the Red Cross in time of war. The Geneva Convention, of course, had laid down specifically the rules governing treatment of prisoners of war, the treatment of the wounded, and so on, and the Swiss, being perennially neutral, are the people best qualified to man the International Red Cross.

Unfortunately, in some of the more recent fracases, some of the countries, even signatories of the Geneva Convention, would not permit the International Red Cross to function. The North Vietnamese government in Hanoi would not even let the International Red Cross into their prison camps, nor arrange for the delivery of food parcels. Their purported reasoning was that the prisoners were not prisoners of war, but war criminals. This is just the kind of thing that can break down the lasting purpose of the worldwide humanitarian Red Cross concept.

Also, each of the 116 countries maintains its own Red Cross Society, and these 116 societies are members of the

League of Red Cross Societies. The headquarters of this organization is also located in Geneva. This League was started by Henry P. Davison, who had been chairman of the American Red Cross War Council in World War I, and who had seen the need for international liaison in the fields of information exchanges and joint action in the event of emergency. This instrument proved effective in recent times in calamities throughout the world whenever and wherever they occurred.

But this is all jumping ahead a bit. Toward the end of World War II, I was still the North Atlantic manager and I had become more and more involved in the all-inclusive American Red Cross family. The head of the Red Cross is a volunteer appointed by the President of the United States, and in those days Basil O'Connor held this office.

The problem we all shared was that we had done our war work too well. The Red Cross had expanded enormously, so much, in fact, that communications between the national headquarters and the chapters had all but broken down. This was all quite natural and was nobody's fault. For instance, I called a meeting of officers of the principal chapters in my area and it lasted for two whole days. We discussed what the Red Cross ought to be after the war, and we had a lot of experience by then, and we came up with some very positive policy opinions. After the meeting, it suddenly occurred to me that it had all been perfectly wonderful. We had taken the Red Cross apart and put it together again and now I had some policy ideas that looked like recommendations. But what was I to do with them? There was no formal line of communication with the national organization along which these recommendations could be advanced as formal proposals.

Shortly thereafter, in 1946, in a personal conversation with Basil O'Connor, I said to him, "The trouble with the Red Cross is that it is running around in a 1945 body, mounted on a 1905 chassis, with creaks and groans and squeaks." He said he agreed with me, and as so often happens when you open your fat mouth, you are asked to do something about it. He asked me to become chairman of a committee of fifty, to review the whole structure of the Red Cross, and to make recommendations for basic changes.

We rapidly mobilized our committee, of whom two thirds were Red Cross people and the other one third were interested members-at-large. We worked on the problems for some fourteen months. We were able to recommend amendments to the congressional charter of the American Red Cross, along with amendments to the working rules and methods.

Our main change was·a recommendation for a new national governing body. The old one had consisted of eighteen persons, one third of them appointed by the President of the United States, with the others chosen on a rather hit-or-miss basis, or so it seemed to our committee. Our new governing body would consist of fifty individuals, eight of them appointed by the President of the United States, thirty to be elected by the 3,500 chapters, and those thirty-eight were to choose twelve more members-at-large, who were to be broadly representative of the public that the Red Cross served. In our language, we were careful to avoid the use of the specific word "representing," because if you represent somebody or something, you build up cliques. If you are a representative of some-body or something, that is quite a different matter.

We made a number of other recommendations and, in 1947, Congress took appropriate action in amending the charter. We were off to the ball game.

When the first election came around, I was elected a member of the new Board, and became chairman of one of the new standing committees, each of which has specific responsibilities in the various fields of operations.

One interesting development came about because we had set an arbitrary quorum for the national governing body. When we set the membership at fifty, everybody said we would never be able to get a numerical quorum, because they would have to come from all over the country. So we set an arbitrary quorum at twenty. But, you know, there never have been fewer than thirty-two in attendance, and we have had as many as forty-eight out of the fifty. This was and is a magnificent indication of the dedication of the governing board members, who do, indeed, come from all regions of our country.

In 1949, when Basil O'Connor resigned, President Tru-man appointed General George C. Marshall as principal officer of our Red Cross.

In his last year, Basil O'Connor had invited me to be the chairman of the national fund-raising campaign. This was a time of some embarrassment because the war had ended just two months after the Red Cross had raised its money for the ensuing year, and this included expendi-tures for maintaining our operations on a full war footing. In fact, the Red Cross had demobilized rapidly after V-J Day, along with the armed services, and we were left with approximately $80 million leftover funds in our pockets. What to do with it? We knew we would never get another nickel as long as people knew we had that $80 million. If we had applied the whole lot all at once, and said we did not need any campaign at all that year, then it would have been very difficult to start the fund raising again in subsequent years. So we had adopted a policy of applying a portion of the $80 million to succeeding annual budgets.

I was therefore able to go to the American people with a rather unusual statement. I said our needs for the year were $81 million, for which we had budgeted, but that we intended to ask only for $65 million by application of the last of our surplus funds. We actually raised $69 million. This was the last time the Red Cross had a really successful fund-raising campaign, not because of my efforts, but because it worked out that way.

My title was Vice-Chairman of the Board of Governors now, and I thoroughly enjoyed the privilege of serving under the former wartime Army Chief of Staff, one of our great military organizers of all time. Not long after the outbreak of the Korean War, President Truman recalled General Marshall to serve as Secretary of Defense and they twisted my elbow for some time, and finally I consented to have my name presented to the President for his consideration as president of the American Red Cross. This was all an unexpected series of events. I had never known General Marshall before he came to work for the Red Cross. He was a compelling man without being austere. He was receptive to ideas. He was remorseless in his rejection of furbelows and fancy stuff. He liked facts, and he dealt with facts. He had a great way with people. In

199

short, he was a great leader, and I cherish the time I worked with him.

I remember when I succeeded him, at the conclusion of a Board of Governors meeting in Chicago, that he introduced me and I responded as best I could. I said something like this: "Have any of you looked at the size of General Marshall's feet? Just look at those shoes! And I am expected to fill them." I thought this was an appropriately humble note upon which to take up my new responsibilities. But afterward, somebody came up and told me, "You damned fool. Don't you know the one thing that Marshall is sensitive about is his feet, the size of his feet?"

On November 2, 1950, President Truman announced my appointment as president of the American Red Cross to take effect on December 1. President Truman commented that General Marshall had done a whale of a job at the Red Cross, and I could not agree more.

At a brief ceremony at national headquarters, General Marshall introduced me to the staff. In response, all I said was, "We are at war. These are days for action, not speeches. I suggest that you and I go to work."

In my first report to the nation as president, I said:

"Korea signaled the end to a hope, and the beginning of a gigantic effort to prepare the nation for defense. The hope was for an immediate, just and lasting peace. Instead, the United States had to take on the burden of strong defense measures and reconstruction in many parts of the world, hoping that tensions would pass, rearming on the chance that they would not.

"With the nation, the Red Cross that had been adjusting its work to peacetime needs turned to the greater tasks at hand. Services to men and women in the armed forces were stepped up because of the great numbers by which the military establishment was increased. The training of millions for civil defense as requested by the National Security Resources Board, in first aid, in home nursing, and as nurse's aides, was instituted. Expansion of the national blood program and the coordination of blood resources for civilian and military needs took place. To help in meeting the needs created by the national and a possible international emergency, the entire organization had to be expanded and adjusted in accordance with its resources. In addition to its defense-geared activities, the normal health and welfare services so familiar to Americans everywhere were continued or adapted in accordance with rapidly changing conditions.

"Each American has a share in the Red Cross. He owes it to himself to know and to make known to others what work has been done with the money, the time and the skills of those multitudes who gave.

"The Red Cross is yours. The Red Cross is more than an organization, more than an agency. It is a spirit, the spirit of the good neighbor, the kind of spirit that prompts people to give of themselves that others may live more wholesomely."

It is twenty-three years since, and I would not change a word of that message.

There was one story from those days about President Truman, for whom I had great respect. Those were the days when we did have television, but without prerecording, and President Truman agreed to kick off our annual Red Cross fund drive in person. That meant "live."

Gladys had been involved in organizing a big to-do in Madison Square Garden in New York City as a kick-off function. Included in the volunteer professional staff for the evening was Margaret Truman, and you know how close Harry Truman was to his daughter.

Well, at the conclusion of the shindig, the television action would suddenly switch to Washington, D.C. There I would introduce the President of the United States, who would spiel his spiel about our Red Cross. The President was in great spirits and there would clearly be no difficulty about the live telecast.

So I was with President Truman in his office in the White House, watching the proceedings at Madison Square Garden on his television set. Even though it was February 28, it was a very hot evening, and all the windows were open. There were a lot of bugs, flies and mosquitoes flying around because nobody had put up the screens. Suddenly, a great big fly landed on Harry Truman's shoulder. I made a pass at it automatically and the President turned away from the TV set. "Roland," he said, "do you suppose that was a horsefly?" I said, "It looked like one to me, sir." The President asked, "Do you suppose it was sitting on a horse's ass?" What I should have said was, "Mr. President, as a loyal Republican, I want to take the Fifth." Instead, I just laughed.

As I have said, Harry Truman was one of our greatest Presidents, and he was a great supporter of the Red Cross. He went out of his way to be helpful as our Korean War expansion moved ahead with efficiency and dispatch.

I was still preoccupied, however, with the modernization of our vast organization, in making it more responsive to the people we served. For example, Gladys was emphasizing, with all her experience behind her, that there had to be basic changes in not only the organization but the whole concept of volunteers. She thought that many of the volunteers were loyal to their own particular part of the Red Cross, while they had little knowledge about the Red Cross as a whole.

Gladys said, for instance, that a Gray Lady who did volunteer work in the hospitals knew little, if anything, of what the volunteers in other programs were doing. Motor corps drivers had been extremely active and valuable during World War II, but they knew nothing about other forms of Red Cross work. So, after the war, all too many of these volunteers thought their work was over and left the Red Cross altogether. If they had known about the other Red Cross activities, they might have been interested in carrying on.

To make a very long story short, we created in the Board of Governors a special committee on volunteers. The chairman was Stanley Hawks, from Minneapolis, and he and his associates worked toward a redefinition of Red Cross volunteers. This was written to be anybody who did volunteer work for humanity through the Red Cross. Since then, all prospective volunteers have been given a brief but profound indoctrination into what the Red Cross is, what all the various services are, what the work opportunities are, and what the role of the volunteer in all of the services can be. When we ask them to choose the branch of the Red Cross in which they would like to work, we know we are not asking a final, exclusive decision. The new volunteers know there are other volunteers doing other things, and they have the opportunity to serve in more than one capacity.

Of course, the demand for volunteer services has increased very rapidly in all organizations in this country. But now in the Red Cross there is only one kind of volunteer, and that is the Red Cross volunteer.

There was another lady whom I wish to mention, and that is Margaret Hickey. She was public affairs editor of the *Ladies' Home Journal,* and still is. And in her own right, she is the vice-chairman of the Social Welfare Committee of the League of Red Cross Societies. She was also one of the members of my so-called reorganization committee in the mid-1940s. Well, she became a member of the Board of Governors, served for two six-year terms, and in later years served also as deputy to the chairman. She represented me in a variety of missions, especially in the international field, and she was able to take a great deal of the load off my shoulders.

Meanwhile, the improvements we had initiated in communications between the chapters, and with national headquarters, were working to plan for the most part. Chapters in Manhattan and Brooklyn in New York City, for example, had previously not been permitted to communicate with one another, except through the area office. Now they can and they do.

Also, one of my staunchest helpers during these days was Walter D. Fletcher, a member of the superb law firm of Davis Polk Wardwell Sunderland and Kiendl, partners of which had been volunteer attorneys during the reorganization. Walter was also my personal attorney. The day the announcement was made of my appointment by President Truman, Walter came over to my office and said, "Roland, I hate the Red Cross because when I was a kid I got a bellyful of it when my mother was chairman of our local chapter. However, I want to be of whatever help I can be to you." I immediately replied, "You have a job as special assistant to the president."

Some time afterward, Walter was officially designated "Special Volunteer Counsel" by the Board of Governors. This brilliant, large, warm, humorous man was always of the utmost help, usually in the background, talking with volunteers and staff and paving the way for the policy changes we were working on, or which I had in mind to propose. He attended every Board meeting and convention, but only once opened his mouth in any session, and that was in response to a direct question.

Walter also attended a large number of International Red Cross meetings and made friends there with many of the delegates and representatives from other nations. Somehow he became friendly with a delegate from Outer Mongolia who spoke no known language. This man's only word in English was "gin." Anyway, as Walter was embarking one day on his homeward-bound aircraft, he saw an individual wildly running across the tarmac. It was the Outer Mongolian, who just wanted to wish Walter a friendly goodbye.

I cannot overemphasize the assistance that Walter was to me for many years in his quiet, effective knowledge of how to deal with people, and how to brainwash them in advance on the changes to be anticipated. It is one of the tragedies of recent years that he died in 1972.

Above all, however, my debt was to Gladys, and this really was a remarkable management relationship. In her position as head of the volunteers in the northeast, and in the New York Chapter, she became very knowledgeable about the workings of the system at all kinds of operational levels. She was also very practical, and was able, by example, to lead the way in what a true Red Cross worker should be.

When I began to have more and more responsibility within the organization, and finally became the head of it, I would really need to discuss the problems at home. I obtained invaluable insight from her, and she was able to help me qualify theory with practical examples. I also think I was able to help her. But, as I said, this was a remarkable team. In fact, it still is.

The last, but not least, reorganizational move I wanted to make was to share my own responsibilities. It had always been my conviction, shared by others, that the principal officer of the Red Cross should be a volunteer, but that there should be a paid line officer with administrative responsibility in a full-time job. At this point, however, I found I was responsible at the Board of Governors level, from which policy emerged, and I was also responsible for the execution of the policy as enunciated by the Board. We did have a nucleus of high-level professional skill available, fortunately, but this was no substitute for a modern, corporate arrangement providing for a chairman and a president.

In 1953, I was granted my desire and I became chairman of the American National Red Cross, with Ellsworth Bunker as president.

CHAPTER X: THE GOOD NEIGHBOR II

President Dwight D. Eisenhower swept into office in 1953 with the reputation of a very good friend of the American Red Cross. He had developed a strong respect for Red Cross people during his Supreme Command of the Allied Expeditionary Forces in World War II. And the President proved almost at once that his reputation was justified.

We had a major disaster, the eastern states floods, in which to my embarrassment I gained a reputation as perhaps the only civilian who refused to respond to a presidential telephone call. President Eisenhower had been in Colorado when the floods struck the eastern states, and he telephoned me at approximately 11 P.M., after I had gone to bed. The maid, unaware of protocol, not to mention prerogative, told the President, "Oh, I'm sorry, Mr. Harriman has gone to bed and cannot be disturbed."

Of course, I called the President the very, very first thing the next morning and apologized. He said, "Roland, how is the American Red Cross flood campaign going?" I admitted, "Not very well." He said, "Do you think I can be of any help?" I said, "Of course you can." The President said, "Suppose I arrange to fly from here, and fly over the devastated area, and then I'll land at the Hartford airfield in Connecticut, and we'll have the governors, senators and congressmen of the affected states there, and we'll have a media hookup." I said, "That would be wonderful."

Unfortunately, it was a very foggy morning and the President did not see very much of the flood damage, but he did make the landing at Hartford. A goodly number of governors, senators and congressmen were there, and the whole idea was to publicize the requirements of how much the Red Cross needed for disaster relief for a fundraising campaign. There were also members of Civil Defense groups there, because at that time Civil Defense had the government role in disaster relief. Former governor Peterson of Nebraska, the head of Civil Defense, was among those present. Their job was to help communities repair or replace washed-out roads or electric light systems and so on, while the Red Cross concentrated on helping individuals.

When the President's plane descended out of the fog and rolled in front of a Navy hangar, all the politicos surged forward. The door of the plane opened and the President's press secretary, James C. Hagerty, emerged. He said, "Will Mr. Roland Harriman and Governor Peterson board the plane." We were standing in the rear, and we plowed our way through the politicos. One of the people I had the pleasure of shoving to one side was my brother, Averell, who at that time was governor of New York. We shook hands with the President and had a quick

9. The author during a moist Spaniel Field Trial at Arden.

10. (*Following page*) Trailing Railroad Ranch cattle to shipping corrals about 1960. Gladys and the author in foreground.

11. Ebby Gerry and the author at Goshen about 1960.

12. Gladys setting world record with Tassel Hanover.

rundown of what we would say on the nationwide hookups.

Governor Peterson spoke about what Civil Defense was doing for disaster relief, and then I explained what the Red Cross was doing and would do. The President ended up with a splendid summary. That night he made a second national appearance, on television from Philadelphia, and he mentioned the excellent work of the Red Cross.

Such was the impact of this extraordinary man that we had, after a few days, to tell the American people not to send any more money. We felt we had all we could handle. We needed $10 million to handle the disaster relief, and the fund zoomed up to $16 million before we could cut it off. This was the only time I ever heard of an organization calling off a successful fund-raising drive. It was a mistake, because a few months later we had some more appalling floods in the western states. Altogether, in these two episodes, the Red Cross invested $31 million in relief and our funds for disaster were down to zero.

Meanwhile, the American Red Cross's other reputation, for immense wealth, was continuing to haunt and plague our public relations. When I was fortunate enough to be able to induce Ellsworth Bunker to serve as president, I called a press conference and outlined the change in the management systems and stewardship. I said, "I know you're going to ask me what Mr. Bunker's salary is going to be, so I will anticipate the question and tell you that his salary will be $30,000." I added, "He, therefore, becomes the largest individual contributor to the Red Cross because he could command a private industry salary in the six-figure bracket."

But the next morning, the New York *Times* led its story,

not with the information that Bunker had become president of the Red Cross, but with the headline RED CROSS PAYS BUNKER $30,000.

About this time, I nearly blew a gasket when I received a letter from a Red Cross chapter chairman in Indianapolis. This man said he had gone to Washington on business, and had taken a rubberneck bus on a sightseeing tour. When the bus passed the Red Cross headquarters, nicknamed the Marble Palace, the tour guide said, "There's the headquarters of the American Red Cross, where they have thirty vice-presidents, each receiving $50,000 a year salary."

The fact was that we had eight vice-presidents and the top salary at that time was, I recall, approximately $26,000 a year.

The Red Cross performed outstandingly in these years in these disaster relief operations. State governments, mayors of cities and county executives named the Red Cross as the official disaster relief agency. But the Red Cross did not do it all on its lonesome. If a disaster was too large for the local Red Cross to handle, we would send in trained professional and volunteer help. We also enlisted the help of other organizations, such as the Salvation Army, who had the desire to help and the knowledge how to help. A number of church organizations were unfailingly helpful and effective. Usually the Red Cross functioned as coordinating agency for all.

There are two segments to every disaster. One is the emergency stage, and the other is the rehabilitation stage of those who have no outside resources. The first entails housing, shelter and medical help. Then the Red Cross helps the victims toward their re-establishment within their community to get them back on their feet with new housing, furniture and equipment.

With the tremendous increase in the cost of rehabilitation in recent years, it has become necessary for the government to enter that phase because no volunteer agencies are capable financially to cope. However, the Red Cross is still recognized as the primary emergency relief agency.

The Red Cross recently has stepped up the activities of its chapters in helping communities to prepare in advance for possible disasters. Much can and is being done, in cooperation with local citizens and local government agencies, so that if and when a disaster strikes, quick, coordinated action can be taken to reduce the suffering of the victims.

The Red Cross got into what we call the blood business during World War II. We were designated by the government to be the official collecting agency for blood to be used by the armed forces medical services. After the war, and after a brief lapse, the Red Cross began to get back into the blood business, this time for civilian use. Other organizations were also getting into the blood picture. Our fundamental policy was, however, that all blood should be donated voluntarily and for free. No donor is paid for their blood by the Red Cross. For many years the Red Cross has provided about one half of civilian requirements.

Many hospitals started their own blood banks, and many communities started their own blood programs. And then too many commercial blood banks started up. The latter paid for donations of blood. Without being unduly critical, I would point out that paid donors tend to come from the less desirable elements of the community. Many skid row people in particular will sell their blood to get money for liquor or drugs.

That was how the hepatitis threat became dangerous, because the need of some of these blood donors for their blood money was so great that they were not apt to be truthful when they were asked about their blood condition. They would even not disclose whether they had had hepatitis or not. It was found that "boughten" blood, so to speak, was fifteen times more dangerous than blood donated freely by volunteers.

So the Red Cross took the lead in espousing the concept that there should be a national blood program. We thought it should be licensed by the government, and that the rules and regulations should be enacted by the government, just so that everybody would be on the same wave length. We also had the safety of the patients in mind, of course.

It is unfortunate that there are still some who drag their feet on what should be an absolutely non-controversial issue, particularly those who make their livelihood out of blood. I am talking not so much about individuals, but about organizations that exist because they get paid for blood. But we are hopeful that there will soon be a national blood program based entirely upon volunteer donors.

The Red Cross, in addition to collecting blood, also spends substantial amounts on research. I never did understand all the ramifications of human blood, and I could not possibly describe them. The fractionation of blood can be used in the treatment of all kinds of diseases, and how to find better uses for blood is one of the principal objectives of the medical and scientific research laboratories. The Red Cross proved helpful in the development of this hopeful trend.

In 1956, President Eisenhower appointed me to another term as chairman. This was the year we had another international confrontation, the Hungarian uprising, one of the most dangerous situations of the long Cold War. In this crisis, the Red Cross was called upon to help resettle some of the Hungarian refugees who poured across the border to start a new life. And, once again, I was moved and impressed to watch my fellow countrymen responding, as they always do, to meet the needs of people in trouble. In fact, it is one of the better elements of humanity that people, whenever their fellow creatures get in trouble, will rally round to help.

The League of Red Cross Societies began their work right at the Hungarian border. We sent one of our top officers over there to help transfer many of the refugees to the United States. It will be recalled that the Congress, in an emergency action, had authorized the admission of scores of thousands of these refugees over and above the usual immigration quotas.

The Hungarians arriving in the United States were assembled at the old World War II Army base at Camp Kilmer in New Jersey. There Red Cross staff members and volunteers were on hand, along with the representatives of the Salvation Army, the church groups, Catholic Charities and the appropriate governmental organizations. The refugees were screened and given the necessary shots. They were interviewed by Hungarian-speaking volunteers and were given clothing and toilet supplies.

Gladys was one of our senior staff at Camp Kilmer and she was impressed by the operation. She thought the food in the mess hall looked wonderful for an Army installation, and the refugees could have anything they wanted. She was also impressed by the fact that the Army was billeting refugee families together at Camp Kilmer, and this was the first time this had been done there.

Gladys commented: "We all felt this is one of the most impressive jobs we had ever seen, from all angles. The Army is doing a superb job, and so are eight separate agencies in addition to the Red Cross. The cooperation between all concerned is wonderful. It is a round-the-clock performance, as planes arrive at all times of day and night.

"The staff of the Red Cross is untiring—the volunteers are standing by in teams, on call at all times. Scheduling all these volunteers has been a complex business, so many want to help, and we have so far met all requests for assistance.

"At Camp Kilmer, we are proving what we have always believed—there is basically just one Red Cross volunteer, no matter what branch of our services, and no matter what the insignia. The whole operation has brought the Red Cross, the military and the community into a closely knit team.

"The other impressive thing is that the refugees seemed to me to be a particularly outstanding group of people. They had risked much, and they all looked well and happy. It was all a very satisfying experience, within the limits of the story of the uprising."

In 1959, I was reappointed by President Eisenhower, as I would be in 1962 by President Kennedy. But our president, Ellsworth Bunker, was tapped to join the Kennedy administration and he was replaced by General Alfred M. Gruenther, former Chief of Staff to General Eisenhower.

General Gruenther was new to me in every way. He was, without question, the best public relations man I ever met. His devotion to the Red Cross was outstanding. He spent a good part of his time, for example, in specifically disproving charges that had been made against the Red Cross. Whenever a criticism of the Red Cross was reported, he would insist on a complete investigation of the facts of the matter. With one exception, he found that the criticisms were unjustified, and he set about obtaining retractions.

Al Gruenther was charming. He was as tough as hell underneath, and he was not enamored of day-to-day administrative work. He liked to deal with people. He had an amazing memory for names and faces. He also had a habit of writing back to people he had met on his travels. Then he would mention in his letters some topic of conversation that had been engaged in. They were never bread-and-butter letters. And Al Gruenther did a lot of traveling, because he liked to get out and about, especially helping build up the morale of the Red Cross "troops."

Upon General Gruenther's retirement at age sixty-five, we were fortunate in obtaining the services of General James F. Collins, a four-star general, a personnel expert at the Pentagon. He was a top-notch administrator, with a good combination of managerial qualities. He worked hard at the job, came up with a lot of ideas and carried them into effect. One program he started was to lay out a five-year plan, something like the Communists', or so it sounds. We knew where we were headed, but we needed some specifics on how we were getting there. General Collins achieved that, and it was a good step forward administratively for us.

Early in the Kennedy years, the Red Cross became engaged in a fascinating and highly controversial activity. Not long after the Bay of Pigs, the Administration had made arrangements to ransom the Bay of Pigs prisoners for $50 million worth of medical supplies and food products.

One day, Assistant Attorney General Nicholas Katzenbach called me up and said he was speaking for Attorney General Robert F. Kennedy. He said they wanted to know whether the Red Cross would take on the job of handling the liaison with Cuba on this matter. He said the government would do its best to secure the gifts from American corporations, but would the Red Cross take on the responsibility of collecting, shipping and arranging for delivery in Cuba?

I thought about it, and said, "Fundamentally, yes." I added that I would have to get my executive committee to approve and he said he understood. He said he would like to come to talk with me and give more details. I said, "Well, I'm out in the country." He said, "That doesn't bother me." He came and we discussed the details. I agreed and we got the proper consent from the executive committee by telephone.

In the workings of this strange arrangement, the Red Cross showed once again that it could function in areas in which the government could not. We did collect the shipments, and we did arrange for delivery. Some of our people went down to Cuba. We were insured by an insurance company in just as unusual a manner. I still have a policy that was written by the president of the insurance company on a yellow piece of foolscap paper.

It was amazing, the reception the goods were given in Cuba, and the only trouble came when, once in a while, one of our manufacturers would unload some of his unwanted and unneeded products. If you can think of anybody who would like a carload of laxative pills, I think we still have some around somewhere.

The Red Cross handled the job expeditiously and ahead of schedule. When we were done, on Christmas Eve, I received a telephone call from President Kennedy from Palm Beach to thank me and my associates, and the whole Red Cross, for the job we had undertaken and brought to a successful conclusion. It was a dandy Christmas present.

In 1965, I was reappointed chairman by President Lyndon B. Johnson, and in 1968, I was reappointed once again. These were the years in which the Red Cross moved once again to support our armed services in a difficult war, in Vietnam. Once again, we did our duty.

In the eight years in which the war raged at a high level, the Red Cross handled over 2 million emergency communications between servicemen and their families. Red Cross field directors and the staff of the chapters at home assisted an astonishing average of 27,800 servicemen every month with personal and family problems. More than 280,000 servicemen participated every month in our recreation activities in Vietnam, at clubs and Clubmobiles, and the Red Cross paid for telephone calls home made by more than 112,000 patients after their evacuation from the front. The Red Cross arranged for the delivery of nearly 3 million Christmas packages to servicemen through the Red Cross's Shop Early Program, made possible by special contributions from individuals and corporations.

At the same time, the Red Cross was expanding its activities closer to home in the field of personal safety. Water safety remained an important aspect of our work. Each year, more than a million people were receiving instruction from the Red Cross in swimming and lifesaving, almost everywhere in America. Almost all the life guards at public and private beaches are Red Cross-trained.

Then the Red Cross intensified its work in cooperation with the United States Coast Guard Service and with local authorities in promoting safety in the operation of small boats. This is more important than it might sound because boating is one of the fastest-growing leisure activities in the country. For instance, I was once asked which of our states had the longest shoreline. I took a stab at California. But it was not. It was Arkansas. There are apparently a great many lakes and rivers and lengths of shoreline in Arkansas, and this state has the longest mileage in this regard in the country. And once I was astonished when, in the middle of the desert at Kingman, Arizona, the gas station at which I stopped for fuel had outboard motors for sale.

At this time, the division of responsibility between chairman and president was working out beyond my best original hopes, and I was proving able to handle my responsibilities in this along with other fields of my activity. But when General Collins reached retirement age, we had a dilemma. At times we had been criticized because our chief executive officer over the years had been a general, a military man. How could this be so when we were a humanitarian organization? That was the specious and unfair question.

Nonetheless, for our next president, I thought we should try to find a civilian, and fortunately we found a man with the ability to lead an organization with a $150-million annual budget and the know-how to work with volunteers. He was George M. Elsey, one of Truman's executive assistants, and one of my brother Averell's assistants in the building of the Atlantic Community, who had worked for the Red Cross before he was lured away to industry. Much to my surprise and delight, George Elsey indicated that he had had enough of industry, and would like to return to public service. So he became the president of the Red Cross, a position he holds to this day.

Incidentally, during these years, a member of our finance committee, who was the chief executive of one of the very largest American corporations, complimented our career staff on their performance and abilities. He said these exceeded anything he had ever seen in America, specifically including his own corporation.

I would add that there were many, many interesting people I met because of my work in the Red Cross. That was one of the great benefits of the association. Gladys and I traveled across the country a great deal on behalf of the Red Cross. We were always warmly welcomed every place we stopped, and invariably, after we left each of these places, we would look at one another and say something like, "Those are the nicest people we ever met."

Not only the Red Cross, but all other good organizations, do-gooding if you like, attract the best type of people. I am not talking about their stature in the community, but just nice folks. This type of work brings out the best in people and that is the one thing about the Red Cross, that there are enrolled as volunteers all kinds of men and women from all walks of life, top to bottom, and I could never know which was the top and which was the bottom.

It was more specifically true, also, that I found the quality of the people on the Board of Governors to be absolutely outstanding, and if it could be believed, this is even improving year by year. At first, some of the chapters nominated some people who they thought were deserving of recognition because of the length of service they had performed in the past. Increasingly, the chapters nominated people who were ready to spend more and more of their time in our actual, current work in an intelligent manner. In any event, I do not know of any finer group of people than the men and women I have met in the Red Cross. This goes for the national headquarters, and in the chapters, all up and down the line.

President Richard M. Nixon reappointed me in 1971, and he was the fifth President to express this confidence. But I was aware that, if I was to carry out my own ideas of good management, I would now have to find my own successor. I started to talk with good people as they became available, who I thought would have the knowledge, ability, interest and willingness to take on a fascinating means of voluntary employment. In each case I was unsuccessful, although I did manage to entice a number of them to serve as at-large members of the Board of Governors.

Finally, in 1972, I read in the newspaper that Frank Stanton was retiring in the following year as president of the Columbia Broadcasting System. The very next day I went over to see him. Frank had a great interest in the Red Cross, and he had done some splendid work for the Red Cross in the media field. Fortunately, I was able to persuade him to have the Board of Governors recommend to the President of the United States that he be appointed to serve in my stead. That all happened in February 1973, right on schedule.

Where, then, did we stand in the American Red Cross after all these years of unstinting effort?

In my final year as chairman, millions of people were helping the Red Cross fulfill its role of the good neighbor. These people, of all ages and interests, representing diverse social, economic and cultural backgrounds, were united in the common aims of helping others and making their communities better places in which to live.

Of these millions of people, more than 36 million were providing financial support. More than 3 million people were contributing blood through the Red Cross. More than 6 million were participating in Red Cross programs in the schools.

Directly, 1,594,020 men and women were serving as Red Cross volunteers, both in the planning and determination of programs, and in carrying them out. A total of just 13,334 career people in the Red Cross were supplying essential staff support.

These were all the people who made up the one Red Cross, the people in 3,177 local Red Cross chapters and in the national headquarters, all of them serving the nation and humanity.

There was even some progress being made toward clearer concepts concerning the United Fund philosophy of donations. The United Fund started out to be the organization that now, in most communities, raises money to support the organizations that the communities want to support. This is now done in one campaign, whereas in the past there might have been as many as fifteen or twenty campagins. The United Funds are a great saver of time and energy and manpower.

Perhaps the greatest change is that, through the United Funds, it is possible to arrange for contributions from salaried employees by means of payroll deductions. There is no way to raise money like a payroll deduction. Roughly, before World War II, approximately one third of charitable money came from corporate sources and two thirds came from members of the public making their own gifts in their own way. Today 90 per cent of charitable money contributed to the Red Cross comes from corporations, officers and employees through those deductions.

One result is that the Red Cross, along with other individual organizations, has lost some of its sense of separate identity. Another result is that we have benefited by far from the ability to raise money from more people than we might otherwise have been able to reach. We have broadened the base of our contributions, we might say, at a cost.

I would add that the Red Cross continues to conduct its traditional March campaign in those communities that are not members of the United Fund, and also in cases in which the United Fund has not been able to raise the Red Cross requirements, and also in special campaigns for disaster relief.

As of now there is an excellent spirit of understanding between the United Fund and the Red Cross on the national level on the basis that we are in partnership in fund raising, and the same prevails in a great number of local situations. But in too many other places there is a lack of harmony to the detriment of all concerned.

This has created quite a storm, and I hope that someday, very promptly, this misunderstanding can be resolved. It is true that there are too many charitable organizations that really no longer have a need, but there are so many more who are doing needed things that nobody should be discouraged. They should not have to get down on their knees and supplicate to be understood. So there is a big problem that is going to face our country for some time.

But there is room for cooperation, as there is in most things. People can give to the United Funds. And they can also give to the organization of their choice.

After stepping down as chairman, I still could not give up the Red Cross, and so I continue to serve as deputy to the chairman of the American Red Cross of Greater New York. Gladys, meanwhile, has advanced to volunteer chairman of Greater New York, and she is also volunteer chairman of one of the newly created regional divisions, which has been named, of all things, the Harriman Metropolitan Division. This embraces northern New Jersey, along with southern New York and Long Island. So she is still very active and her reputation is such that her advice and counsel is keenly sought.

She has her office at Red Cross headquarters in New York City and she spends a lot of time at it, and gets a great deal of enjoyment out of it. She is my age, and her vitality is high. But to sum it up, she is the practical member of the Harriman Red Cross team. The difficulty with any organization is that people get together in a smoke-filled room and decide on policy, and they do not know whether or not that policy is workable. By my own experience, plus what I learned from Gladys, I was able in those smoke-filled rooms to be helpful in adopting policies that were workable.

In my own case, after retirement, I received generous citations, letters, certificates and so on. Throughout these reminiscences, I have shied away from mentioning the nice things people have sometimes said about me, but I will let the formal presidential statement into the record. It read:

"For almost a quarter of a century, your immense dedication to the well-being of your fellow man has been matched only by your distinguished and imaginative leadership of the Red Cross activities which have touched the lives of nearly every American throughout the land.

"Beginning with your initial appointment in 1950, your stewardship has guided the Red Cross through one of the most trying periods in our nation's history. Yet at every turn, whether in the wake of natural disaster, in the upheaval of great social crisis, or in the turmoil of two major wars, the Red Cross has never failed to meet the challenge with vital and timely assistance, and unfailing compassion.

"During this time, under your sure direction, the Red Cross has continued to grow and change with the country, taking on new duties, meeting new responsibilities, and bringing new benefits to those in need and distress."

I was also privileged to receive a citation from the Pentagon, and after the ceremony, I was asked to say a few words. I said I had the Red Cross very well organized, because the volunteers did all the work and I received all the glory. But I had been the head of the greatest volunteer organization in the world.

I said I had more people under my direction than the Secretary of Defense had under his. But as the armed forces were rapidly becoming a volunteer organization, I took it upon myself to give a word of advice.

I said, "You can't tell a volunteer anything, but if you can once get out in the lead ahead of them, then prepare to run like hell to keep from being trampled from behind."

But I think the thing that has pleased Gladys and myself the most is the establishment by the National Red Cross of an award, a silver medallion with her and my profile on it, given each year to the outstanding Red Cross volunteer in the country. It is called the Harriman Award.

CHAPTER XI: THE COMEBACK OF A SPORT

Originally, the principal thing that attracted me to Elbridge T. Gerry was that he was born when I was twelve years old. I thought it was wonderful to be an uncle at that age. I was extremely proud. I used to stop at my sister Cornelia's house during the holidays and get acquainted with Ebby.

Then, later on, Ebby became identified with the Central Hanover Bank in New York City and he did very well there. Without Averell and I having anything to do with it, the other partners at Brown Brothers Harriman & Co. said that we ought to get Gerry into the firm. We did. He worked in the firm in various capacities with distinction for a number of years, and was made a partner. His subsequent leadership in our business community needs no comment from me, and as chairman of the executive committee of the Union Pacific Corporation, he has shown statesmanlike qualities of a very high order.

Now, Ebby had also been a polo player, and his interest in horses centered on that. He knew of my interest in trotting, and he finally came to me and asked if I would buy him a colt, so he could have a trotter. He was saying that I was a good judge of horses, I suppose, but I replied, "That would be like committing suicide. If you buy one colt, you would be perfectly sure of failure."

I continued, "I tell you what I will do. I usually buy four yearlings every year, and after I have bought them, we will put the names into a hat. You can draw one of the names and you can pay me what I paid for it."

Well, the first year Ebby drew the next year's two-year-old champion. The second year Ebby drew, not the champion, but the ranking champion. At that point, I told Ebby, "Here's where we stop. No more drawing of names out of a hat. From now on, we are partners."

Well, the Gerry luck rubbed off on the partnership called the Arden Homestead Stable based in Goshen, New York. The Stable has since had an unparalleled record as the home of world champion trotters. In the thirty years since 1944, the Stable has owned and raced six out of the only thirty-seven trotters who have covered a mile in 1:58 or faster since trotting history began.

All six of our Arden trotters were world champions. They were: Titan Hanover, 2, T2:00, 3, T1:58, the first 2:00 two-year-old (1944); Star's Pride 1:57.1 and Florican 1:57.2, fastest race trotting stallions (1952); Matastar, 4, T1:55.4, fastest four-year-old trotting stallion (1962); Florlis, 3, 1:57.3, world record for three-year-old trotters when made (1963); and, in 1973, Flirth, 3, 1:57.1, the fastest race trotting gelding ever.

Of that collection, four—Florican, Matastar, Florlis and Flirth—were Arden homebreds. No other breeder, I am told, large or small, had ever been credited with so fast a quartet of trotters. And racing your own horses, the ones you breed, this is really the fun of the game. Many years ago, an old-time breeder told me, "Roland, you'll get more fun seeing a horse you bred come in third, than a horse you bought come in first." And he certainly was correct. We have been lucky enough, and breeding is mostly luck.

Let us now get Ebby's and my own roles and responsibilities out of the way, so we can get on with it and talk about trotting. I was a founder of the Trotting Horse Club of America, also chairman and now honorary chairman of the United States Trotting Association, chairman of the Board of the Hambletonian Society, president of the Hall of Fame of the Trotter, past president and now a vice-president of the Grand Circuit, also president of the Orange County Driving Park Association, which operates the Historic Track at Goshen, New York, not far from our home at Arden.

Ebby served as treasurer of the United States Trotting Association, president and director of the Standardbred Owners Association, director and treasurer of the Hambletonian Society, treasurer of the Hall of Fame of the Trotter, and also vice-president and director of the Orange County Driving Park Association. Ebby's distinction was recognized when he was appointed the first chairman of the New York State Harness Racing Commission.

Of course, the explosive growth of harness racing in the United States is now a part of our postwar history. Among the influences were the Phillips' Starting Gate, a novel, folding fence on the back of a vehicle, which solved the problem of the false start, also the legalization of parimutuel betting in New York State, and also the establishment of the Roosevelt Raceway at Westbury on Long Island.

In terms of attendance, betting, purses and tax revenue, harness racing by 1950 was ten times larger than it had been a decade earlier, and by 1960 it had more than doubled again. A million-dollar gate in boxing was considered a big deal not very long ago. Even by the early 1960s, harness racing tracks contributed sixty times that amount just in the payment of taxes to the governments of the host states.

Now, let me make it clear that I have no objection to anybody in trotting making a lot of money. The sport is now so big we really have no total idea of how much this is. After all, I spent a great part of my life and a good deal of my own money keeping the sport alive and helping make its current success possible.

Somebody once said to me, "Roosevelt Raceway has saved trotting and ruined it. The Yonkers, too." Well, that is not so. They have saved trotting, and changed it.

I like the people who run Roosevelt and Yonkers. They honestly and sincerely try to put on a good show. But it is very easy to forget that trotting is a sport, and to think of it only as a revenue-collecting instrument for the states is not right. That was why I objected so strenuously when the New York State Harness Racing Commission barred children from the tracks.

I thought that was terrible, and I said so. I feel the only way to gain enthusiasm for any sport is to initiate people into it when they are young.

When Ebby was chairman of the Commission, I remember before one meeting at Goshen, he came to me and said, "Unc, one of the rules is that children are not admitted." I said, "Yes, and I disapprove of it greatly, because they are our future patrons. They are the future

owners and spectators." Ebby, who was no sympathizer
with this rule, said, "Anyway, you're going to have to kid-
proof the Historic Track."

I went to a great deal of trouble to put up wire fencing,
even across the windows of the stabling that faced public
property. When the meeting opened, there was not a kid
in sight. About the third race, however, there was an accident on the backstretch, and within moments, literally
moments, at least three hundred kids appeared out of
nowhere, racing across the infield toward the scene of the
accident. How they got in, where they came from, why
we had not seen them before, remains a mystery.

I am glad to say that this rule was amended to permit
youngsters to attend when accompanied by parents or
guardians, which really meant any visible adult. Now the
kids are back.

Trotting has always been a very important part of my
life. My father was a trotting enthusiast, and he had many
good trotters and pacers, including a couple of world
champions. He founded Arden Farms, the lineal ancestor
of our Arden Homestead Stable, long before the turn of
the century. Many famous horses were bred or owned by
Arden, with Billy Andrews as the trainer. These included
the trotter Stamboul, 2:07-½, who is now buried in the
Historic Track infield, and John R. Gentry, p, 2:00-½, the
little red horse who should have been, in the opinion of
many, the first 2:00 standardbred.

There was once an important race at Goshen, but the
train that could get my father from New York in time was
only permitted to stop in Goshen to pick up passengers
for Chicago. So my father wired a friend of his in Goshen

to go down to the station and buy a ticket for Chicago. The train stopped at Goshen and my father got off in time to see the race.

Another time, in the winter, my father sent a message from New York to the stables that must have sounded like some old-fashioned espionage. The message read, "Send Stamboul." The stable promptly dispatched the champion Stamboul to the city, where my father wanted to hitch him to a sleigh to race on the Harlem River Drive, then known as the "Speedway." This is now one of our bumper-to-bumper automobile drives.

There used to be a great deal of that type of informal racing on country lanes and roadways. There was also nothing more pleasant than driving a horse in the country on quiet roads. The last time we did it, really, was during World War II, when we had gasoline rationing. I had an old set of harness in the stable, with an old buggy, and I brought down two of my trotters and hitched them up. I used to drive around the countryside, drive down to the station in a horse and buggy the same way my father had at the turn of the century. It was fun.

After my father's death, my mother maintained the family interest in the sport. I think I really inherited my love of the trotting horse from her. We used to have amateur races at Goshen every Saturday afternoon during the season, and whoever was in the house had to go. There was no question about it. They had to go to see the races.

I remember one time, in her later years, she would sit on the lawn at the foot of the stretch at Historic, with her two little white terriers and her parasol, and she would watch the races from there. One time, a pet colt of hers was declared not to be the winner. From where she sat, it was definitely the winner. Fortunately I was with my mother, because she jumped to her feet, parasol and dogs and all, and started to cross the racetrack to tell the judges what she thought of them. I was able to catch her just in time.

I was driving regularly in matinees at Goshen by the time I was fifteen or sixteen. The first trotter I drove was a mare my mother had bred named Quisetta, and she was a quitter. She would go like a house afire and then just give up. I had to learn to sprint with her from the start and get a lead, and then try to hang on until the end. It worked. I won my first cup with her for most races won in the matinee season at Goshen.

My greatest thrill was when I bought my own first trotter, called Jean Oro. She was a little black mare and I won the season's trophy with her for winning the most races at Goshen.

Arden Homestead Stable, as my stable was now known, was very successful in the 1920s under our trainer Billy Dickerson. We had such stars as the world champion two-year-old Peter Maltby, Guy Ozark, Guy Trogan, the 2:00 pacers Anna Bradford's Girl and Highland Scott.

Nationally, however, the sport was in trouble, with purses small, attendance low and most of the action confined to county fairs. Another difficulty was that the rules of trotting were interpreted quite differently by three different organizations that held sway in different parts of the country. If some man disobeyed a rule and was expelled from the East, all he had to do was to go to the Middle West and continue to race out there.

Finally my trainer came to me and said, "Roland, let's

get out of this racket." I remember saying, "Billy, before we quit, let's see if there isn't something we can do about it." Little did I know that I was sentencing myself to fourteen years at hard labor.

But in setting out to do something about it, I called a few stalwarts together and we created what we called the Trotting Horse Club of America. It had no powers except those which were self-imposed. But the first thing we did was to buy Wallace's Register and Year Book. These were the all-important volumes that contained detailed breeding and racing records that were absolutely vital to the sport. A man named Best and his wife had been trying, unsuccessfully, to keep track of all the breeding records, issue all the breeding certificates and maintain the records of the few tracks that were still operating. Chaos reigned.

So, in 1923, we bought the Register Association, which had even stopped publishing, and we moved it to Goshen with a wonderful editor named Will Gahagan in charge. We put up funds to support some of the traditional events, and inaugurated some new ones. Meanwhile, the Hambletonian Society, separate from the Trotting Club but drawing its support from the same people, set up the Hambletonian Stake. This became the most important trotting race in the United States.

The Trotting Club did much to revitalize the Grand Circuit, the major league of trotting, by helping some of the Grand Circuit tracks that were in financial trouble. Sometimes, we subsidized the meetings.

Most importantly, we used our efforts to get the three governing bodies to work together. The National Trotting Association ran things east of Ohio and on the West

Coast. The American Trotting Association had most of the Middle West. The United States Trotting Association governed Ohio. They resented the devil out of us because we had the idea that a new association should represent all the people in trotting—owners, breeders, drivers, everyone, not just the track operators who were the members of the existing organizations.

We were making headway after about ten or twelve years, but only slowly. I was talking to Will Gahagan of the Register and the Year Book and I said, "Will, those buzzards have split again. Let's forget the whole thing and go about our business." But Will replied, "No, let's have one final whack at it. Let's have a meeting and invite folks who have anything to do with trotting. Let's call the meeting the Friends of Trotters, at Indianapolis. We'll get a man named Leo McNamara. He is a well-known breeder in that part of the country. We'll get him to run the meeting. You can play it from the sidelines."

On October 24, 1938, I sent out a telegram of invitation that has since been described as the wire that saved trotting. It read:

RECOGNIZING THAT IN THE PAST FEW YEARS MANY PROBLEMS HAVE CONFRONTED LIGHT HARNESS HORSE RACING CONCERNING WHICH THERE HAS BEEN MUCH DISCUSSION BUT LITTLE ACTION MAY I HAVE PRIVILEGE INCLUDING YOU ON COMMITTEE FIFTY BEST FRIENDS OF TROTTING TO SPONSOR A NATIONAL GATHERING AT INDIANAPOLIS NOVEMBER 11TH TO 13TH TO DISCUSS THESE MATTERS FOR THE GOOD OF OUR SPORT AND TO RECOMMEND

SPECIFICATION THEREON STOP NO OBLIGATION
OTHER THAN YOUR MORAL SUPPORT AND ASSIST-
ANCE STOP KINDLY WIRE VIA WESTERN UNION
ACCEPTANCE STOP THANKS

E ROLAND HARRIMAN

About three hundred people came to this meeting at
Indianapolis, at their own expense. Everybody just got up
and had their say. We insisted that we *had* to work this
thing out or the sport would go down. The way to put the
sport back on its feet was to have a single governing body.
We said to the three organizations, "You fellows either
join up or else." We talked and talked, and finally everybody agreed to agree. We did it by exerting the moral
pressure, really, of all of these men gathered there. The
officers and directors of the three regional associations
finally saw the writing on the wall.

It was after this meeting that I received the greatest
compliment I ever got in my life. A young fellow came up
to me, and he said, "Mr. Harriman, I can't wait to get
back to North Dakota and tell those fellows there that
you're not the son of a bitch they think you are."

So the old trotting associations disbanded, and came
together as the United States Trotting Association.

The United States Trotting Association set its first annual budget at $39,000. Today, the USTA budget is $2.5
million! On top of the $39,000, however, we recognized
that we had to have somebody to sell the USTA to the
rest of the trotting public, and to run the organization itself.

There was a man by the name of Frank Wiswall, a lawyer in Albany, New York, a very competent man who had been active in racing all his life. So we scratched around and found another $20,000 to help induce him to become president. And he did a great job of work, traveling all over the country, bringing the good news about the USTA to everybody, and he was very well accepted. People seemed to want to clean up the mess that had bedeviled this sport for twenty or thirty years.

Well, the USTA was formed just in time, because in 1941, the New York State Legislature passed the parimutuel law permitting betting. After that, in pretty quick order, a number of other states passed similar legislation.

Needless to say, I was delighted when the states usually adopted, as their code of rules, the USTA rules that we had developed over what seemed like many years. There were some exceptions.

Actually, it was a close-run thing. Although the Historic Track held License #1, both from the USTA and from the New York Racing Commission, the track that first operated under the new parimutuel law was Roosevelt Raceway on Long Island. It was due to open on a Saturday night, and was supposed to have eight races with no fewer than six horses to a race. Horses cannot race more than once a week, or should not. This meant that for a full week's program, the number of horses on hand would have to be eight (races) times six (horses) times six (nights), whatever that is. By electronic calculator, that is 288.

Well, there were not nearly enough horses on the grounds at Roosevelt on that Saturday night, but luckily it rained, and the first Saturday night program was washed out. By Monday night, the management of the raceway was able to get enough horses on the track to put on a night's racing. That is, forty-eight horses. The start-up was as close as that.

Under this original parimutuel law, incidentally, the number of tracks that were permitted to operate in the state was eight. The length of the race meeting was limited to a relatively short period time, say, thirty days, and the number of races permitted to be run each day was limited to eight.

Now, there are still only eight tracks licensed, but with the encouragement, in fact with the persuasion, of the state, the season has been extended to the middle of January until Christmas, from the middle of May to the beginning of November.

All of this has meant that the breeding has increased fantastically. Years ago, there were perhaps three stallions standing in New York State. Now there are more than three hundred. The number of registrations for breeding purposes or racing purposes was perhaps three thousand horses. Now, there are twelve thousand or fourteen thousand, and so it goes. The number of owners, horses, stables and tracks around the country has just boomed upward, sometimes with good results and too frequently, I am afraid to say, with poor results.

Sometimes I think the sport is vanishing, and now we have just another business. But I also think the pendulum has swung too far in the wrong direction, and someday it will swing back to normal. I have not the slightest idea how this might happen, but this is usual with things in this world. They swing back and forth, from one end to the other.

238

One of the reasons for the increase in popularity of trotting is that, in many states, such as New York, Illinois and Ohio, some races are limited to horses that have been bred in that state. For instance, in New York, they have what they call the New York State Sire Stakes. That means the sire must be standing in New York State when he is bred to the mare. The mare can be shipped in from other states, but the stallion must be standing in the state.

I was asking my manager at the track how he accounted for the increase in betting at the Historic. He said, "Well, that is very simple. In the old days, a stable would come in with a single owner and perhaps ten horses in the stable. Now, one horse will appear with ten owners."

Of course, the betting at the Historic Track is picayune by comparison with the giants. We bet in one week of our racing just about as much as they bet on a single race at Roosevelt. But I like that, because we still have a Historic Track that is historic.

For example, we have heat racing at the Historic, which is practically non-existent elsewhere. And people come to the races because they want to see the horses race. They are interested in the horseflesh. The heat racing is a carry-over from the good old days. Then a horse would have to win two out of three, or sometimes three out of five heats, and because of that, the trotting horse won a great reputation for stamina. However, the betters want to see fresh horses in each race, so the big tracks have gone to a one-dash system. Some of the trainers have fallen for this, and they do not want to race more than one dash any more.

I would also like to mention another thing. It comes

through when we are talking about pacing. There have always been pacers. In fact, this is almost a breed separate from that of the trotter. But more and more, because of the increase in the number of races, also in the size of the purses, the owners and trainers want to get their horses into the winner's circles as quickly as possible. In the old days, they were more patient.

I can remember a way-back story, that trotting was a manufactured gait at speed, and you have to take time to get a horse to the races, you have to shoe him right, you have to do all sorts of things to get him to trot fast.

Well, for some reason or other, the pacing gait seems to be a more natural gait than the trotting gait, and so many of the trainers nowadays take drastic action. When their pupil horse seems a little backward on the trotting, they just slap these hopples on them, and tie their legs together, and they go to pacing and develop much faster.

As I say, the pace seems to be an easier gait, and it is more popular with the betters, because a pacing horse is less apt to break stride, as they say. If you break stride, you have to pull the horse up until he gets back on stride, in which case he has probably lost the race. So the pacers run truer to form than the trotters, because they have less opportunity to break stride.

The only difficulty is that when they do break stride, they often fall down and take the whole field with them. This is a dangerous thing, and an ugly thing, and an artificial thing, and that is the reason why the Harriman-Gerry stable never has a hoppled pacer. They are just as beautiful horses, just as well-bred, everything else—except that because of the impatience of everybody these days, they use these horrible contraptions called hopples.

I hasten to say that I still get a thrill, a great thrill, when I go to the races, and particularly at the Historic Track. I also have an interest in, and helped start, the Saratoga Raceway at Saratoga Springs, where the sport is also conducted for sport's sake.

I sold the one-mile track at Goshen, the Good Time, to William H. Cane, the man who built Boyle's Thirty Acres, the site of the Dempsey-Carpentier fight. Bill Cane was a terrific supporter of trotting, and the Hambletonian was run at the Good Time for more than twenty-five years. It cost Bill a lot of money to keep it there. After he died, Yonkers Raceway, in which Bill had had an interest, wanted to move the race down there. But the conditions of the Hambletonian call for it to be run in the daytime, on a mile track, and in heats. Yonkers could not meet these conditions and, to cut a long story short, the Hambletonian was moved to the DuQuoin Fair Grounds in Illinois and Good Time became a training track.

Later, in 1947, the Trotting Club sponsored the publication of an authoritative history of the sport by John Hervey, whose experience took him well back to the early days of trotting. The book was an outstanding success and is still a textbook for the sport. We wanted to illustrate this book with appropriate photographs and found that about the only ones available were in Mr. Hervey's own collection. This made us realize that the memorabilia of trotting were fast disappearing.

So the Club members decided to encourage the establishment of a trotting horse museum in Goshen to be known as the Hall of Fame of the Trotter. In 1951 the museum opened with its home in the famous Stony Ford

Stables, which made a most attractive and appropriate location.

After that successful effort, it was decided to liquidate the Club as having achieved its main purposes. I have always had a horror of useless organizations retaining their existence, so, like the National Economy League, the Trotting Club, in 1961, was given a decent burial. All its last remaining assets were transferred to the Hall of Fame of the Trotter.

During these years one of the unexpected things that happened was that Gladys became one of our great champions. "I never knew anything about trotters before I met the Harrimans," she said not long ago. "I had to learn in self-defense." She had beautiful hands and a good seat in the sulky, and she could rate a horse to perfection.

Gladys, in fact, was the first woman ever to drive a horse in 2:00, which is roughly the equivalent of running a four-minute mile. It was at Good Time Park in 1929 that she drove the free-legged pacer Highland Scott, p, at T1:59-¼. Twenty-one years later she hung up another world record with the three-year-old free-legged pacing filly Tassel Hanover.

Gladys wrote for the magazine *Country Life:*

"It is with the greatest pleasure that I watch the expression on the faces of my friends when I casually remark that I have spent the morning in helping to train our trotters and pacers.

"Almost invariably a rather startled, pained look creeps over them, and they say, 'You mean, you were sitting in one of those funny little two-wheeled carts with your feet up in the air and holding yourself in by the reins? Isn't it fearfully uncomfortable? How many times did you fall out before you learned? Is it really any fun?'

"Fun—of course it is fun, providing you love horses . . . One day Mr. Dickerson, who trains our horses, seeing that I was in riding clothes, asked me if I would care to drive one of the horses a slow mile. In fear and trembling, I climbed into one of those funny carts, and away I went. At the end of the mile, I was entranced, speechless with joy . . .

"The first few times one drives, it really seems as if nature had not provided us with enough hands. After getting arranged in the sulky, someone will quite firmly offer you the reins, a whip and a stop watch. The latter, they proudly show you, has a split-second hand, and you are expected to drive your mile according to the pre-scribed schedule, catching each quarter and sometimes the eighth of the mile on the watch, punching it casually with your left thumb at the correct moment.

"After a few struggles, when you are sure the watch will drop and the reins will slip, in spite of the handholds, or the whip will fly away in the wind, it suddenly all seems very easy and nat-ural, and you find yourself timing your heats with not only ease, but accuracy, and not even noticing the other articles in your hands.

"As a starter, aged horses are the more com-forting to drive. They know what is expected of them and in many cases have as much, if not more, intelligence than many trainers. Next, you will find the younger horses entrusted to you, and this is fun because you can actually see them improve and learn to do what is wanted of them. Finally comes one of the most exciting moments that I think one can experience—driving a horse for a fast-time record. To be official, this must be done at a recognized meeting, before timers. As two minutes and a fraction constitutes very fast time—and only twelve people have ever driven horses in less than two minutes—it obviously is not something accomplished every day.

"I will guarantee you a reall thrill when the moment comes and you, with a 'prompter' running beside you, leave the wire, and you hear that fatal word 'Go' fairly shouted at you by the starting judge. You know you are in for it. The realization sweeps over you with staggering vividness that should you make a sudden move, be it ever so slight, or twitch a muscle in your hand, or if those hooves that are pounding along in absolute one-two-three-four rhythm make a misstep, spoiling the complete harmony, you are ruined. You know that every second represents forty feet of ground.

"Then comes that last quarter of the mile when you must bring your whip into play in order to urge your horse to exert every ounce of his strength. It seems like eternity as it all must be done from the wrist, tapping him steadily, yet not changing the pull on his mouth by too much motion of the hand, which might cause him to break when he is so tired.

"It is a tense few seconds, both of you working together, and the harmony must be complete. And after it is over, I guarantee you will never have lived through a longer or more exciting two minutes. The sensation of speed, combined with the absolutely perfect coordination a horse must have to actuate such time, is inexpressible."

While still active, head trainer Billy Dickerson recruited a young fellow named Harry Pownall to drive a fast, temperamental young filly named Farr in the 1937 Hambletonian. Farr finished 4–2 to Shirley Hanover and divided second and third money with a colt who finished 2–4. Harry Pownall succeeded Dickerson upon the latter's retirement, and Pownall trained Titan Hanover, Florican, Star's Pride, Tassel Hanover, Matastar and Florlis. Pownall also figured as a kind of straight man in an article that Robert Creamer, of *Sports Illustrated,* wrote about me in 1962. This was how the article went, in part:

"Harriman looked at Pownall appraisingly. 'You got a horse for me to drive?' Pownall said. 'Well, I think there's something we better talk about.' Harriman smiled again. 'I know all about it,' he said, 'and it's all right.' Harriman had undergone an operation during the winter and had been cautioned to take it easy for a while.

"'You sure?' Pownall said. 'I've got my orders.' 'I'm sure,' Harriman said, 'It's all right.'

"They walked out to the sunlit stable area and Harriman watched as the crack four-year-old Matastar was hitched to a sulky . . . Then he climbed into the sulky behind Matastar. Pownall walked alongside and said, 'About :23, :25.' Harriman nodded and took Matastar slowly along the track the 'wrong' way, jogging him for a while. Then he turned him, and brought him down the track and past the starting post.

"'Is that the boss out there, Harry?' a stable-hand asked. 'Yep,' said Pownall. 'What's he going in?' 'About :25.' 'He looks pretty good.' 'He sure does, and it's the first time he's been out this year.'

"As Harriman completed the second tour of the half-mile track, Pownall said, almost to himself, 'Right on it, 2:25.' Harriman brought the horse back to Pownall, who walked up, touched his watch, and said, 'Right on the button.' 'Had to walk him the last quarter to do it,' Harriman said.

"A trotter came jogging along the track driven by a man in a sulky who held a small boy, no more than three or four years old, on his lap. The boy's eyes were brilliant with excitement. Harriman watched the horse and the man and the boy move slowly down the track. 'That's what I mean about trotting,' he said."

The trainer who succeeded Harry Pownall on his retirement was Ralph Baldwin, who took the job after years as a public trainer, as Two Gaits Farm trainer, and after a spectacular time with the large Castleton Farm Stable. Baldwin promptly upset the favorites and set world records with a trotting gelding who had previously made only nine starts with four wins prior to the big race.

Flirth, 3, 1:57.1, is one of only four trotters ever to win the Hambletonian who did not race as a two year old and the only gelding other than Greyhound to win the Stake. Flirth's final heat of 1:57.1 exceeded Greyhound's previous all-age gelding world marks, and its time of 1:57-¼. Flirth's two heats at 1:58.2 and 1:57.1 were a two-heat, all-age world mark.

As I mentioned before, if you are lucky, you can buy a great trotter. If you are very lucky, you can breed one. As *The Horseman* virtually exulted:

"Look at Flirth!

"His sire is Florican. His dam is the Arden Homestead mare Mirthful. So Arden bred Flirth, bred his sire, and owns his dam."

Florican, the oldest of all the Arden homebred champions, probably ranks as our all-time favorite. I think one of my greatest thrills in harness racing since I won as a teenager came when Florican was the world's fastest trotting stallion for twenty minutes. He beat his stablemate, Star's Pride, in 1:57.2, only to be defeated by that great Arden trotter in 1:57.1 in the very next heat. These were surely the greatest pair of trotters ever to race for one stable in the same season, and in one race to set two world's records.

Star's Pride, incidentally, went to stud at Hanover and is now the all-time leading sire of 2:00 trotters with 23, in addition to five 2:00 pacers.

Florican, now twenty-seven years old, stands at Castleton Farm. He is the sire of four 2:00 two-year-old trotters, more than any in the history of the sport, and his eleven in 2:00 are all trotters.

But in trotting, sometimes, I do not want to be up to date. Sometimes I like to look back, to lose myself in cherished memories.

One such memory is forever recorded in an article written for the local paper by Elizabeth Rorty, a top turf writer, who used to live in Goshen. It goes:

> "The bay mare stamped impatiently as the driver slid into the sulky and tossed her head as the loose check rein was fastened. 'Let her walk along, Lou, she wants to go,' and off went Tassel Hanover, almost dancing, through the drawgate and out on to Historic Track. The morning was crystal cool and clear and the air was like wine. It was such a morning as Goshen seldom sees in August.
>
> "The grandstand was empty, the barns were empty, and only six people saw Mrs. Harriman's last ride with Tassel. The track was like brown velvet, smooth and resilient, responding to Bud Kidney's careful grooming after the rains earlier in the week. Bud was there watching, and Dick Mitchell was cooling out little two-year-old Impkin, the only other horse on the grounds. Bo Gill and camera took some shots for the record. Up in the old judge's stand, Mr. Harriman held the watch.
>
> "But there were no cheering crowds, no

music, no banners, no excitement. There was just Historic Track, and we were up from Arden to work Tassel, just a lone horse and driver, training a mile on a deserted racetrack.

"Tassel jogged past the wrong way, at a free swinging trot, curving her neck and bouncing a bit. It was such a lovely morning. Looking at her, so dainty and delicate, it was hard to realize the steel and whipcord muscles beneath the shining silky coat, until you remember that mile Tassel did in 1:59-⅕ at the mile track the previous week.

" 'How fast will she go, Lou, do you suppose?' 'Not too much, maybe 2:06 or 2:07, I guess. She raced pretty hard last week. Mrs. Harriman will probably let her go along about where she wants to.'

"Tassel scored down again, shifting into a pace as she picked up speed. On the soft brown track, her hooves scarcely made a sound. By the old Cox barn, she pulled up, and came trotting back. The driver nodded to the judge in the stand. The next time would be it.

"Back past the little audience on the rail by the drawgate she trotted, still prancing a little, feeling good, ready to go. Nobody said anything. It was so quiet you could hear the faint whir of the well-oiled sulky wheels, and the rustle of the maple leaves as a light breeze stirred in the paddock.

"This time when Tassel turned, there was no doubt about it. She shifted to the pace as she turned, and was in high gear as she passed the stand. Flat and sweet and straight she went away, and as she leaned into the first turn— 'They're on their way,' said Bud.

"Round to the quarter she went, and the silence was queer, somehow. Time seemed to be standing still, and only the little mare was moving. She swung into the stretch, and still you could hardly hear her, so smoothly, so effortlessly she went. Her driver sat still, yet imperceptibly the mare went faster and faster. Into the turn and on into the back stretch, she seemed to be floating, yet must have been flying to get there so quickly.

"Past the three quarters and round the last turn—no banners, no music, no crowds, no other horse to prompt her—down the stretch came Tassel, with only the light hands and low voice of her driver to bring her home. Lovely Tassel, finishing her last mile for Mrs. Harriman, pacing like a champion, pacing as if she loved to go pacing by herself.

"She flashed past the wire at better than 30 mph, then slowed into the turn. From the judge's stand, an incredulous voice went down the track —'2:03.' And back came Tassel, trotting up to Lou to be unchecked. She would not wait for pictures, and neither would her driver. 'Don't stop her now, Lou, she wants to get back to the barn.'

"Tassel was glowing, and so was her driver. She was the picture of a racehorse, looking ready for more miles, faster and faster. Her nostrils were wide, her eyes were flashing, her step was quick and strong. Mrs. Harriman took a long look as Lou led her away. And that was all for Tassel that morning at Historic.

"Tassel held then the track record for pacers at Historic, shared with The Tippler, at 2:01-⅖. But the few who watched that mile in 2:03, done so easily, so effortlessly, every quarter faster than the one before it, wondered how fast Tassel could have gone that lovely morning.

"There is always a day for a champion, when the weather is right, the track is right, and the horse is right, and that is when world records are made. It was that kind of a day for Tassel at Historic and, in a way, it was a shame no one will ever know how fast she could have gone.

"At Historic last week, she gave her driver a mile to remember—probably the easiest mile in 2:03 ever paced on a half-mile track."

CHAPTER XII: PARADISE

I would like to tell a story about the history of Arden, particularly for my grandchildren and my great-nephews, not to mention any others who might be interested. I will have to go back a little bit into the history of Orange County, as I understand it.

This part of the country is underlaid by a series of iron deposits, running from the north central section of New Jersey, up through the Ramapo Hills to the Hudson River just south of Newburgh, New York. There were a number of successful iron miners in this region from the days of the earliest settlements. Among them was the Parrott family, and they must have started operations midway in the eighteenth century. They had a holding of approximately three thousand acres, with a number of mines located on it. This was on the west bank of the Hudson River.

Another member of the Parrott family had a foundry at Cold Spring, on the east bank of the Hudson, which must have been in operation well before the Revolution. The iron for the famous chain that was laid across the Hudson to keep the British fleet from moving upriver was mined at Arden, which was then called Greenwood Furnace. The links were cast in the Parrott foundry at Cold Spring. These were rather ponderous links, some of which are still exhibited at West Point. They were about two feet in length, and very thick.

After the Revolution, the iron in this district had considerable economic importance for us, as it supplemented imports from Europe. The Parrott family again became quite famous during the Civil War. One of them, a West Point graduate, was the designer of the Parrott fieldpiece that was widely used in the Union Army throughout the conflict. Not long ago I was given a model of the Parrott gun. I, in turn, gave it to a museum at Cold Spring, where it will be permanently exhibited. I am told the Parrott gun was to the Union Army roughly what the French 75-millimeter gun was to the Allies in World War I.

The Parrott family got into serious financial difficulties about 1880. The iron mines in this part of the country were marginal at best. They were high grade in the quality of their ore, but the deposits were rather limited, and comparatively expensive to work. Then came the opening of the great Mesabi Range in Minnesota. The Mesabi offered the opportunities of massive production and quick, convenient transportation. The Parrotts and other miners in this part of the country were faced with ruin.

Sometime in the 1870s, my father, before he was married, had become friendly with several of the residents in Orange County. Among them were the Parrotts, and he used to visit them at their home at Greenwood Furnace. There still is in Arden Village, as it is now called, the remains of a furnace. There is also a more dilapidated ruin, of another furnace, just below the dam of Echo Lake.

The string of three lakes north of Arden were dammed up for water supply and all through the woods you can still find leveled-off spots where charcoal was made. Other relics are the remains of quite a large settlement, which numbered, I am told, something over two thousand people who had been engaged in the making of charcoal, the mining of ore, and the smelting of iron in the furnace.

Now, when the Parrotts got into financial difficulties, they came into serious arrears in their taxes. In 1886, their property had to be put up at public auction by the sheriff to meet back payments. My father, as a friend, attended the auction. The only bidders were, I am told, not miners, but lumbermen, who clearly had their eyes on the forests on the property. This disgusted my father, because he could not abide any thought that the landscape was going to be ravaged. On the spur of the moment, he put in a bid, and it was the high bid. The Parrott property was knocked down to him, about nine thousand five hundred acres of it, for $52,500.

The first thing that happened as a result of the fortuitous bid was that the Parrotts never spoke to him again, and became his bitter enemies. Their theory was that, if my father had not spoken up, others would have stayed in the bidding and the price would have gone much higher. In fact, I have seen an estimate prepared before the sale of what they thought the property was worth. This estimate was something over $100,000. But this estimate reflected an assumption of a profitable iron business, when the opposite was the case.

The Parrotts did reserve from the sale some fifty acres

on which their family houses were located. They stayed on living there while my father and mother moved in as neighbors. My parents occupied on weekends a small, three-room house just across the road from the Parrott homestead.

My parents became increasingly fond of the locality, and they began to spend more and more time at their cottage on the shore of Echo Lake. When their children were born, they gradually enlarged the original shack, from room to room, from story to story, until it was a rambling three-story frame house. With the growth of the family, and with the encouragement our parents always gave us to bring friends for the weekend, an additional building was constructed to house the bachelor guests. It had a squash court, a billiard room and other facilities.

After my father settled in, he began to buy up farms and woodlands around the original Parrott purchase. This protected his holdings, but that was not his main purpose. These were the early days of the conservationists. My father was one of these who envisioned that a large metropolis such as New York would have to have much more breathing space in the future. He was a strong supporter of the move to create what later became the Palisades Interstate Park. After his death, my mother carried out his wish by presenting some ten thousand acres of land and a million dollars to the state of New York to be incorporated in this beautiful park. It is now known as the Harriman section.

Then there were other iron mines in the region, over at what is called Sterling, west of Arden. My father acquired this Sterling mine, which was still in operation in 1900, and continued to be worked through World War I. At the start of World War I, the Sterling mines were leased to the Midvale Steel Company, which took over the operations. This company was absorbed by the Bethlehem Steel Company, which built quite a village, of several hundred houses, to be occupied by their employees.

After the war, however, the demand for iron ore dropped off once again and the Bethlehem people exercised their right to cancel their lease. They even moved all their buildings away, with the exception of a large fieldstone schoolhouse, which is there today.

There were about twenty thousand acres of forest land connected with the Sterling mine situation, and it became quite a burden on us to protect it, to pay taxes on it, and to manage it. So we finally sold this land in the 1950s to the City Investing Company, which has started a very fine development there. It is now the site of a number of laboratories run by universities and corporations, with each laboratory maintaining buildings where the researchers and other employees live. They are doing an excellent job of it, and they are good neighbors. Once again, a Harriman property has wound up in good hands, for good purposes, rather than in the hands of irresponsible real estate developers.

My father also started a dairy business at Arden, and we used to grow fodder for the cattle, hay and so forth, and we used to supply not only ourselves and the villages around us, but also the nearby community of Tuxedo Park. This was quite a complicated business in the horse and buggy days. Tuxedo Park was about seven miles away from the dairy, and we had to carry the milk down to a substation on the outskirts of Tuxedo Park. Delivery wagons would take the milk to the homes of our customers.

Later on, we supplied the United States Military Academy at West Point and we had a little industry on our hands. But our costs were more than we wanted to handle, due in part to our proximity to the metropolitan area, and we gave it up a few years ago.

In this regard, my father, in the '90s, tried to distribute some of this milk into the poor districts in which the Boys Club of New York had been active. He insisted, years ahead of his time, that the milk should be distributed in what would now be called sanitized containers. In order to ensure that the milk would be purchased and given to the children, he sold his milk for a penny a quart below the market. Unfortunately, however, the poor people were suspicious. They would not buy cheaper milk because they felt there had to be something wrong with it.

My father also installed a small, water-driven electric power plant in the village of Arden. This was meant to supply electricity for all the neighboring families. Later, when a greater demand for electric power developed, he built a coal-operated power plant in the nearby village of Turners. This supplied power to the whole community, and the power was transmitted over lines to the Sterling mine for use in the industry there.

In time, a local utility company opened up in the town of Monroe, next door, and when this became operative it was much larger than ours. So we closed our power plant down and the building is now occupied by a chemical company, which is a substantial local employer. The Monroe power plant was subsequently absorbed by a larger utility company, and its plant stands idle on a standby basis.

After my father's death, the villagers of Turners changed the name in my father's honor to Harriman, which is the sign now emblazoned on the direction plates of the New York State Thruway. One claim to fame that the old Turners had was that the first train order by telegraph was issued from the Erie Railroad station there. A plaque on the station commemorates this important event.

Another point I would mention, somewhat out of context, is that my father built a new road along the west side of the Ramapo River. What we now call the Valley Road used to be a public road, a segment of the Albany Post Road. This section crossed the Ramapo and Erie at Arden, ran on our side of the valley, and exited at Peckham's Pond near Central Valley. Another branch turned left at what is now known as the watering trough, where it joined the westbound highway. After my father had built the new road, he exchanged it for the old road.

Finally, in the early 1920s, I bought out the rest of the Parrotts. Much of the old hostility was gone, and, as a matter of fact, I used to play with some of the children of the Parrott relatives, and we got on well.

The road that passed the old homestead, and now runs through the courtyard of the present Arden Homestead, used to be a public road. There was a little community named Baileytown about four or five miles up the valley. After I had bought the Parrott land, Baileytown and some of the other private properties in that area were merged into the Palisades Interstate Park, and eventually there was nobody but Harrimans living on this road. So we got permission from the county officials to close it.

Meanwhile, the Palisades Park all around us became

one of the most popular state parks in the nation, just as my father and the other conservationists had envisioned.

Almost every weekend and during the summer months in my childhood we spent at Arden in the old house. The house had great charm, and there was nothing luxurious about it. It was a comfortable, old-fashioned country home. There were a lot of nooks and crannies. It was a wonderful place to be extremely young.

This reminds me of something that was rather important in those days. I went to a children's party where they had a prestidigitator, and of course, he pulled the usual rabbit out of the usual hat. I was sitting in the front row, watching with rapt awe, and by golly, when he pulled the rabbit out of the hat, he gave it to me. I brought it home to Arden and I remember, over all these years, that the rabbit's name was Tommy. I used to keep him in the stable, and I fed him every day. I even persuaded my mother to buy him a wife but fortunately all around nothing happened.

My first real effort with animals at Arden was with chickens. One summer, together with adult assistance of one kind or another, I built a chicken coop for my chickens. I had six or eight. I had a wonderful racket going. I would feed the chickens with my father's corn in the stable, and then my mother would buy the eggs. I think this was on a very good economic principle. If I had one egg, I was paid five cents. If I had two eggs, I was paid four cents per egg and so on. So I had no costs, I earned some money and I ate the eggs.

Unfortunately, Echo Lake in front of the house was not really suitable for swimming, because it was very shallow, with a muddy bottom. But Forest Lake about three miles away in the woods was another matter. This lake was ninety feet deep, entirely spring-fed, and it is a beautiful body of water about three quarters of a mile long and about a half-mile wide, with a couple of islands in the middle of it.

We would go up to Forest Lake, put the horses in a small stable that was there, get in one of our boats and row over to one of the islands. We used to spend many nights in the so-called Adirondack type of camp, tents with wooden floorings, and from our island base we would swim and fish to our heart's content. We would cook our own meals, of course.

I remember my father sitting on the dock in a small camp chair. He never brought much work home with him in the way of papers, but he spent a great deal of his time at Arden thinking. He would sit in that camp chair for hours at a time. He would have a little fishhook dangling over the side into the water. I do not think he ever caught any fish that way, but I imagine he caught a lot of fish mentally.

Another thing I remember about this lake is my father's sister. He had loaned her a house about a half a mile from ours, and she and her husband lived there. His name was Charles D. Simmons. I learned only some years ago that he had been a manager in the original firm of Brown Brothers. He was also the father of E. H. Harriman Simmons, who became president of the New York Stock Exchange.

Uncle Charlie Simmons used to ask me to go fishing with him in Forest Lake. In those days, fishing consisted of what they call "still" fishing, as compared to casting for fish. You just took your boat out to a part of the lake where you felt there might be a fish. You would anchor, and then you would sit out there in the broiling sun with a rod over the side, probably a bamboo pole with a frog on the end of the line. You would wait for the fish to bite.

Uncle Charlie said that if you made a bit of noise, you would scare the fish away. So we would sit in the broiling sun for two hours or more, and I was not allowed even to scrape my feet on the bottom of the boat. Talk was out of the question. After a few more experiences of this kind, I declined politely to go fishing with Uncle Charlie.

There were lots of differences in sport in those days. One thing my father did was to teach Averell and me how to shoot. He taught us the proper way to handle a gun, never to have it loaded in the house, never to have it cocked while you were walking and never to cross a fence without opening the gun. These and other sensible safety precautions seemed normal to us then, but they are now few and far between.

My father was a great walker and I used to go walking with him and perhaps one of his house guests, and they would talk, chew the rag, and I would skip around with them. It was all just a normal family relationship, as was practiced in those days. We did not have to be with one another, or accept one another's company. These came naturally to us.

Similarly, I did not realize at first that we were living amid absolutely beautiful scenery. I did not realize it was beautiful because I did not know what was not beautiful. At Arden, as a child, I appreciated everything. I knew that everybody did not have the same opportunities I had, so I did appreciate it. But I think I only really recognized the full beauty of Arden after World War I, when I had been away from it for a long time. I was happy to get back to Arden, to all its freedoms. Until then, it was like asking, "When did you realize how nice and soft your bed was?"

As we always had in New York, we did everything at Arden on weekends and during the summer holidays as a family. On Sundays, we would have breakfast at 9 A.M. Of course, I was up before that, running around doing something. Then, as in New York, I would have to learn the Collect for the day before I could read the funny papers. At 10 A.M., I would hitch up my pony and wagon and drive to church for Sunday school. At 11 A.M., the rest of the family would arrive for the morning service.

Then we would return to the Homestead for lunch. We always had meals together there, as in the city, and there was one taste of my father's that I particularly disliked. We both liked baked apples, but he would not let the cook put a drop of sauce on them. I liked mine running with juice. But I got dry apples.

I had a dispensation from the school in New York City that I could be a half hour late on Mondays. So, on Mondays, my father and I used to catch the 8:08 A.M. from Arden to Jersey City, and we crossed the Hudson by ferryboat. One ferry ran from Jersey City to lower Manhattan, in the vicinity of Chambers Street. Another went up to Twenty-third Street. My father would take the lower Manhattan ferry and I, along with the other members of the family, would take the ferry to Twenty-third Street.

There we would be picked up by the family's electric brougham. I wish we had them now. It was slow, but there was no noise, no fumes, no pollution. It was very pleasant. But it was the end of another weekend.

Through a great many of these early years, or so it seemed, we were in close contact with major construction projects at Arden. First, I used to ride with my father with a team of trotters all through the woods at the time when he and my mother were looking for the right location for their final home. He was no respecter of terrain and we almost went up and down precipices. Later came the opportunity to rubberneck as my father had roads built and improved. They were excellent roads, coiling around the hills at near-level gradients. This was the principle he had employed in the expansion of the Union Pacific, and he used it close to his new home. In fact, the county erected a small monument on one of those roads, reading in part: "He built level roads in hilly country."

There was never too much doubt where the new home would eventually be placed, because my mother was adamant that it be located in a beautiful setting right on top of a mountain. My parents' instructions to the architect, Thomas Hasting, were that the height of the mansion must be kept as low as possible so the house would not disfigure the mountaintop.

A number of my parents' friends were building châteaux of French or Italian design, or imported English castles. But my parents, who had great faith in America, decided that everything in the new Arden House would be American. There would be American materials, American art, American workers on the construction project, everything 100 per cent American.

A shop was built at the foot of the mountain, where everything was put together for the house. The walls of the house were the stone that was excavated from the foundation. All the marble, the wood, the carving, was indeed American, and this was a great boost to American artists and designers at a time when almost everything good was supposed to come from abroad. And a funicular railway was built up the side of the hill, with a car pulled up and eased down by cable. Men and materials zoomed up and down the hill in a transportation device straight out of Switzerland.

Soon, a pair of narrow-gauge rails ran from the railroad station to the foot of the hill. We had a wonderful contraption, a gasoline-driven motorcar, and we used it on this narrow-gauge railroad. The contraption would meet us at the station and it would roll along the tracks to the foot of the funicular railway on which it was hoisted up the mountain. Then there were also rails running from the top of the funicular railway into the back yard of the building, Arden House.

Another thing we used to like to do was to go riding up there. The horses would be brought from the stables at the foot of the hill, transported up the hill on the funicular railway, and we would ride away through the forests.

The cornerstone of Arden House was laid in 1906 but it was mid-August 1909 before we actually moved into the livable portion of the house that had been finished. Unfortunately, my father died some three weeks later and he never had more than a glimpse of the wonders of the place. It was not until three or four years later that the building was really completed. Also, the workshops at the foot of the hill caught fire and burned down during the final phases of construction, so there was a further delay in completion.

It is a very large, very rambling mansion, but my mother had a great knack of making things homelike. In those days, there were also plenty of servants. Every room was filled with flowers, every room was always ready for occupancy, and we young people were encouraged to bring our friends to the new house. Frequently, we would sit down to dinner with anywhere from ten to twenty people.

There was what we would now call a great deal of youth activity and the only trouble with the place was that we were on the top of the mountain. It was difficult because when we wanted to see other people, or do anything outside, we had to go all the way down the mountain. It was three miles by road from the top to the valley, and this did restrict our association with the local youngsters.

On the other hand, we were now closer to Forest Lake, which was only about a mile away from the house through the woods, and there was even more reason to go swimming and fishing. We had a tennis court there and we used to enjoy that. My mother was very keen on croquet and she had a croquet court on one of the lawns of the house where we used to engage in not very friendly rivalry. My mother believed that the game should be played strictly by the rules. So everybody got to the point of carrying a rule book in his hip pocket and cited the proper authority when anybody was suspected of transgressing. It never came to blows, but some of the croquet games had their moments of argument about the rules.

One of the principal features of Arden House was a

massive hall dominated by an organ. My mother loved music, and fortunately a good organist lived nearby. He used to come over and play, as I recall, for as long as two or three hours. My mother used to sit and listen, do needlework or something of the sort. One of the nice things about the organ was that it had a player attachment. You could play rolls of music on it, like a pianola. That was good fun and you could pull out any stop you wanted. My favorite was a deep roar.

My mother loved the house and she realized her and my father's ambition in that it really is a tribute to American design. The art, painting, carpeting, tapestries, furnishings of every nature were American-made, with a single exception. There were no manufacturers in this country of really high-grade linens. So my mother had to compromise and furnish the linens from abroad, from Ireland, I believe.

And after Arden House was finally completed, my mother was concerned about the designers and craftsmen who had done the job, and whether they would be able to find good work. So she formed a corporation known as the Harriman Industrial Company, and the talented people who had helped build Arden House stayed together and designed and built and furnished other dwellings in Orange County. Only many years later, as the older designers and craftsmen died or retired, did we suspend this operation.

Now, when Averell got married in 1915, my mother made available to him one self-contained wing of Arden House. Averell and his wife lived very happily in their end of the place and my mother lived in the rest of the house, and they never got in each other's way unless they wanted to. The scope of the house can perhaps best be illustrated by describing a party Averell gave a long time afterward, over a Thanksgiving weekend, when he decided he would fill every bed in the place with a friend. For weeks afterward, people would meet one another and say, "Oh, you should have been at Averell Harriman's Thanksgiving party." They would reply, "But I was there. I didn't see you there."

Until I got married, I had a room at Arden House, a kind of bachelor arrangement which could be shut off from the rest of the house. One of the three so-called bachelor rooms was usually filled with my guests, not continuously, but for weekends and in the summer.

My three sisters each had a suite of their own, with bedroom, sitting room and bath. But it did not seem to affect them any, all this deluxe atmosphere, and they all just had a good time. The house really lent itself to being used by different people doing different things. Nobody got in one another's way, nobody got in each other's hair, even though we did always meet at mealtimes, as we had when my father was alive.

My mother was described in her biography, *Mary Williamson Harriman*, by Persia Campbell, as: "Essentially modest with respect to her low voice and, except with her family and a few close associates, personally reticent, even shy. Her rather formal pattern of living provided, in a sense, a shield against intrusion . . . Tall and slim, always dressed and coiffed with simple elegance, her distinguished bearing led people to move aside for her when she attended public functions.

"But her personal revelations showed that beneath her

outward reserve there was a generous and kindly heart. A clear, incisive mind was enriched by a shrewd sense of humor. Her strong will tended to skirt public controversy and underlying her attitudes and decisions was a deep religious spirit expressed not only in churchgoing but also in the personal consolation she found in biblical sayings as she quoted in her diary, and also in the lyrical quality of her expressed feeling for the varying rules of nature."

The Arden staff party in the church at Christmas time was quite something, and at one I remember, there was an attendance of 188 children, 25 mothers and 65 men. That is an indication of the number of children there always used to be around Arden. They and their mothers would fill the pews of the church to overflowing, and the men would also be standing in the back of the church.

Averell and I and some of our sisters would invariably attend these affairs, and we would help in giving out oranges and cupcakes to the children. Every child got a toy of some description. We had a wonderful lady who lived in Arden named Mrs. Budd, who helped my mother, and personally selected all the toys we gave out at the staff party. The most popular gift was a pair of ice skates. In those days, we did not have the skates attached to the shoes as we do now. We had skates that clamped on to ordinary shoes, with a locking key. The mothers would get handkerchiefs, and the men would get woolen gloves.

It was really quite an occasion, and the staff party was continued as a family tradition until well into the 1920s. By this time, we no longer employed nearly as many people, and more and more people were moving elsewhere.

My mother also made September 9 a wonderful occasion for all of us. This was the anniversary of her wedding, the day before the anniversary of her bereavement, and so she decided that we would all celebrate Family Day on September 9. Later, we called it Harriman Day. All the members of the family tried to get to Arden House from wherever we were. We all had fun and frolic together, with nothing gloomy about it, a nice family reunion, and we all spoke to one another for hours on end and enjoyed one another's company.

At one of the first Harriman Days, when I was a little older, I remember my sister Mary told me that my father, as he was dying, realized that it was his thirtieth wedding anniversary. My father knew that the jewel for the thirtieth anniversary is the pearl, and he worried that he had not got a pearl to give to my mother.

Fortunately, however, Mary was a very sensible girl and she had gone out on her own and bought a pearl so that he would have one to give to my mother. My father said to Mary, "I haven't got a pearl to give to your mother." Mary said, "Oh, yes you have," and she handed him the pearl for his last anniversary gift the day before he died.

One very pleasant aspect of Harriman Day was that my mother used to give us little trinkets after dinner, some of the small treasures she had. One year she outdid herself, and this was before gift tax days. She presented each member of the family with a piece of jewelry from her own collection and this was quite an occasion.

It was against that, a few years later, that she dug to the bottom of her safe deposit box and got out all her worthless security certificates to give us. But I was fortunate. I got twenty-five shares in a cemetery. Until the state took the cemetery over some thirty years afterward, I received a dividend each year.

In the meantime, our beloved old homestead, down by Echo Lake, had been vacant since 1909. When I got married, in April 1917, my mother gave it to me along with approximately eight hundred contiguous acres. When Gladys and I returned from Santa Barbara in 1919, we began to refurbish the place. It was still in good physical shape, and my mother also gave me much of the old furniture that had been kept in storage. The only difficulty Gladys had when she began to arrange the furniture in the house was that various members of the family would come down and say, "That piece was not there. It was over here." Invariably, after the family visitors had left, Gladys would move the piece of furniture back to where she wanted it.

Incidentally, Gladys got on well with my mother, who respected her many qualities, not the least her candor and truthfulness. Once Gladys was asked by my mother to view a new marble bust of my mother by Malvina Hoffman. It was to be placed in Arden House. But Gladys did not hesitate to tell my mother that she did not think the bust was good enough. My mother had not been well and Gladys thought the bust reflected this. Gladys was right.

So we had the lovely old rambling solid house, but it began to have its drawbacks. Serious drawbacks. For example, rats would get into the walls somehow, and die there. We had a terrible time discovering where they were and removing the remains. This was before we had scientific rat exterminators. Whenever we thought we should rebuild, however, we would decide against it, because it was such a wonderful place. We agreed to stay there and make the best of it. But one night, while Gladys was in her bathtub, the plaster ceiling fell down on her. That settled it!

We had a great time at Arden as young marrieds. One of our favorite games with our friends was hide-and-seek, and another was sardines. Sardines was played when one member of the party hid, and everybody would have to find him or her, and as soon as the person was discovered, the discoverer would hide in the same place until there was a big crowd there. There was no winner. The loser was the last one to find the sardines.

I remember one night, it was rather late, and after we had been playing sardines for a while I was "it." I hid myself in our double bed. I remember the horror of the rather prim young lady guest who discovered me. She did not quite know what to do about it. But she was a good sport, and she climbed in, too.

Another of our guests hid in an old-fashioned shower bath that was really just hung over the bathtub, with a curtain around it. He was fully clothed, I hasten to say. There were two or three people already with him when I found the sardines, and I turned the shower on.

We were all young, and the great winter sport was not skiing, but coasting. There were some wonderful hills all around to coast down on old Flexible Flyers. This would not be very popular today because the only way to get another coast was to climb up the hill again with the Flyer and come back on down.

We also had a toboggan slide up the side of the hill beside Echo Lake. We used to shoot down on toboggans and keep on sliding right across the icy lake. That was quite exciting, too.

In those days, there was still quite a large community and everybody seemed to have large families. Shades of Planned Parenthood, there were three families in particular, one with fourteen children, another with thirteen, and the third with eleven. When these families got together, there were usually enough youngsters around to play two or three hockey games all at once.

I was also fond of baseball, and although I was not any good at it, I did help organize a kid team in Arden. The villages around also had kid teams, and they were something like the present Little League. But the only trouble was that, as soon as I got everything organized, I was fired off the team because I was too inept as a player. But I am sure we had just as much if not more fun than the Little Leaguers today because there were no anxious fathers who made a great to-do if their children lost. I think this might have been several years earlier, but everything at Arden seemed to fit into one continuous and overlapping memory.

Arden was only fifty miles from New York City but it really was a wild place, and still is. It teemed with deer, and when we were more bloodthirsty, we used to enjoy deer hunting during the season. As a matter of fact, the white-tailed deer group in the American Museum of Natural History was obtained at Arden.

We used to have a duck drive, and for this we had to have a pond, and we had to raise ducks, mallard ducks. They were fed up on the hill above the pond, and they were released. They got into the habit of flying back to the pond. The trick was to put our guns in blinds between the hill and the pond and, as they flew over, to take pot shots at them. This did not deter our ducks from flying back to the pond, however, but it did teach them each week to fly higher and higher. This we carried on until World War II.

The country surrounding Arden was alive with ruffed grouse. They would go in cycles, sometimes very plentiful and sometimes scarce, and we used to enjoy walking through the woods with our dogs, flushing and shooting ruffed grouse. This led us gradually to pheasants, which we would buy when they were young, rear and liberate before we went shooting. Subsequently, chukar partridge and bobwhite quail were treated in the same way.

Of course, in all this activity, we had to have dogs. Averell was very lucky. He imported a Labrador bitch around 1930 and bred her to an American dog. Her puppies became champion retrievers in field trials, which were then very popular, and the strain from old Peggy is still considered the top strain in this country.

One time when we were grouse shooting in Scotland, all of our friends filled their bags much more than I did, because they had dogs. So I sent a telegram to a man I knew who raised cocker spaniels in the southern part of England, and asked him to send me a dog. He replied that he only had one puppy and he was only six months old. I said to send him along.

They say, to every man comes a great love. All I can say is that mine arrived in a crate. He was somewhat—although I was his master and he attended me most—he was rather fickle with his attentions, until one time we were out shooting at Arden and I dropped a bird on the ice on a stream.

Danny, the cocker, went after it and fell through the thin ice. There was only one thing to do, and I did it, and that was to make my way out through the ice to rescue him. It was only thigh-deep for me, but it was about twenty degrees and when I got out I was mighty chilly. So was he.

From that time on, Danny never left my side. Gladys and I wanted to breed more Dannys. So we sent word to my friend in England, and he sent over a bitch we called Pat. Her real name was Merlin's Mistletoe. And I had the same record as Averell, because from that mating we produced many champion English cocker spaniels in this country in the field trials.

We still use the dogs for shooting and, more important, for companionship, and the dogs are a really fundamental part of our life at Arden. When there is no season for shooting, our pleasure is always just to walk, and it is always more fun to have dogs walking with you. The dogs accompanied me when I went fishing even, and every time I hooked a fish, the dogs were delirious with joy.

On June 1, 1932, my mother wrote a letter to Laura Fraser: "I am reveling even on this gray, chilly day at being at Arden, feeling much better and more independent than in the city . . . My best at Arden is always better than my best in New York."

In her last letter to Mrs. Fraser, dated October 27, 1932, my mother reported that she was planning to move from Arden back to New York City. She wrote that she was looking forward to a lovely weekend at Arden, with the colors still all around. She wrote, "I am hoping to enjoy these few beautiful days in October, with pleasant memories to treasure next winter." A week later she was undergoing an emergency operation at New York Hospital. The attempt to save her was in vain, and on November 7, she died.

A tribute to my mother had been paid by Chancellor Elmer Ellsworth Brown on the occasion of the presentation to her of an honorary degree of arts and letters by New York University. The citation read: "You have yourself, in these later years, carried weighty responsibilities which you have discharged with fidelity to your own high sense of stewardship; patron of science in fields most closely related to the betterment of human life, patron of art and music and religion, friend of boys, friend of artisans, friend of those in need of friends."

When World War II had come along, Averell loaned Arden House to the Navy as a recuperative hospital, and it remained so until after the war. Then Averell began to have the idea that the house should continue to be used for a constructive public purpose, and I could not have agreed more. So Averell had several long talks with General Eisenhower, who was at that point the president of Columbia University. It turned out that General Eisenhower was working on another idea, that it would be very fruitful to have a series of gatherings of top-flight brains in the country to discuss current events. This would be called the American Assembly, and the intellectuals would be able to get together for several days at a time, absolutely undisturbed, to hash out their ideas of what should be done about the problems.

Well, the two ideas jelled, Eisenhower's and Averell's. Of course, Arden House was an ideal place for an American Assembly. When people get to the mountaintop, sometimes they literally cannot get away, unless they want to walk the three miles down to the valley. One visitor said, "It's a wonderful place, but the front stoop is awfully high."

So in 1951, Averell transferred Arden House, together with some acreage, to Columbia University for use by the American Assembly. It became known as the Harriman Campus of Columbia University. The Assembly only met three or at the most four times every year. Columbia had the vision, the typical vision, to use it throughout the year for educational purposes, both commercial and private.

Columbia now conducts courses there during the summer months for junior officers of corporations, for example, so they might learn some of the intricacies of corporate management. This is such a successful operation, so I am told, that reservations sometimes have to be made three years in advance.

The American Assembly idea has spread throughout the country. The Columbia American Assembly at Arden House selects the subjects to be gone into, prepares background information, invites participants and runs the show. Then Columbia makes all this data available to interested organizations everywhere in the country. The result is that Junior American Assemblies are now held in a great many of our cities and the basic idea looks better and better.

So Arden House has become, much to Averell's delight, and mine, a national institution. It is being used in accordance with my father's philosophy, for a useful purpose.

Averell, as the reader of any newspaper is aware, is still going strong, and he is one of our national assets. He will soon turn eighty-four. Although Averell lives in Washington, he continues to maintain a house on the Arden property and he keeps his voting residence there. His children are bringing up his grandchildren at Arden, also.

I mentioned that, many years before, the plaster had fallen on Gladys in her bathtub at our old homestead residence, and that we had reluctantly decided we would have to rebuild.

So we employed an architect by the name of Julian Peabody, who was an old friend of the family, who knew the way we liked to live. It did not take him long to draw plans according to our specifications. We wanted a place somewhat in the old tradition, where we and our two daughters and our friends could live. We wanted it right on the site of the old homestead, right beside Echo Lake. Since 1925 we kept it filled with our friends and our daughters' friends in the Harriman tradition until our two daughters married and moved away, but we still enjoy a very warm, a very comfortable, a rambling kind of place where the two of us can rattle around.

Inevitably, too, our clutter of assorted souvenirs and possessions has surrounded us, and we love this feeling. Fortunately, Gladys and I have similar tastes. Just as I have given her pieces of silver at Christmastime, or pieces of Steuben glass, she has given me little statuettes, some of them by the very great western artist Charles Russell and others by the Frasers, Jim and Laura. None of these are of any size—we can put them on the table at Arden Homestead, and they are not overpowering. Everybody can look at them, and we can look at them. At the moment, the most famous thing at Arden Homestead is this past year's Hambletonian trophy.

The Harriman oak, as we call it, still stands beside Echo Lake as it has stood through so many generations.

As for the whole Harriman property at Arden, I own certain acreage and Averell owns certain acreage. I have given some of my acreage to my surviving daughter, Phyllis, and some to one of my grandsons. Averell has given substantial acreage to his two daughters. But we all still use the land as if it was one place. This is still the Harriman home, and it is available to all the family for whatever enjoyment we can get out of it.

I have a problem with our own home, however, which is too large for a modern generation to live in and maintain, and too small for a major organization like the American Assembly. But I have found that my friends at the New York Hospital would like to have a place in the country where some of their doctors and researchers can meet in seclusion the way the larger gatherings meet at Arden House. The idea is basically for a boy-size Medical Assembly. So I have arranged that, when Gladys and I are though with the place, these medical people will have the first choice of occupancy.

Now, if this New York Hospital idea does not work out, then our trustees are instructed to find some other public use for our property. We are just not going to let it get into the hands of some get-rich-quick real estate developer who would clutter up the beautiful countryside with cheap claptrap cracker boxes.

As I reach the end of my reminiscences I want to record a couple of episodes which I remember about my relationship with my father. In June 1909, he and my mother traveled to Bad Gastein in Austria, hoping the doctors and the waters there would help the intestinal troubles which were bothering him and from which he was to die a few months later.

During July two of my sisters and I joined them. One day, my tutor, a guide and I took a hike through some rugged Alpine terrain and we came down to a village about five miles from the hotel. There we stopped and had some hot chocolate. I remember the guide said, "Don't you want to hire a carriage to go back to the hotel?"

I said, "My father always taught me to finish what I started." So we set off, and it was a very weary twelve-year-old kid who climbed the last half mile from the valley up to the hotel.

I remember my father took me to task about this, and he said, "I'm told that you walked home because you were afraid of me." I said, "No, that's not quite true. But you always taught me to finish what I started, and I tried to do what I thought you liked and wanted me to do." He said, "That's all right, just as long as you weren't afraid of me."

And then there was one very real statement my father made that I have remembered and tried to live by. Just when he said it, and under what circumstances, I do not remember.

What he said was:

"Leave whatever you touch better off for having touched it."

And, I must say, it has been a lot of fun trying to carry out that principle.

I think it is a very good principle.